"Practical, encouraging, honest, touching and amusing. Ellis[on?]
loves children and shows her readers why she and they ca[n ...].
— Joe Nathan, Director, Center for School Change, Humphrey Institute of Public Affairs, Univ. of Minn.

"A cornucopia of provocative ideas and timely classroom tips."
— Howard Gardner, author of *Frames of Mind: The Theory of Multiple Intelligences*

"Launa Ellison's classroom is electric! The excitement of children discovering answers and coming up with questions is palpable. It's important for teachers, parents, and administrators to see behind the scenes of a supportive and challenging learning environment which is based not only on how learning actually occurs, but on how adults can use their own 'magic glasses' to perceive the real needs and possibilities of each child."
— Dorothy Fadiman, Producer of the PBS special *Why Do Kids Love These Schools?*

"An outstanding sourcebook on how to meet all children's learning needs. Launa Ellison's classroom is one every child deserves to experience."
— Bernice McCarthy, author of *The 4MAT System*

"This book fills an enormous gap. Parents, educators, policy-makers all over the country want to know if the new learner-centered ideas really work in the classroom — how and why they work, and what they look like in action. *Seeing With Magic Glasses* fills this need beautifully."
— Peter Kline, author of *The Everyday Genius*

SEEING WITH MAGIC GLASSES

A Teacher's View from the Front Line of the Learning Revolution

·∞·

Launa Ellison

GREAT OCEAN PUBLISHERS

ARLINGTON, VIRGINIA

With thanks to all of the children who have taught me,
especially Chris and Jennifer.

-∞-

Permission for the use of material from the following sources is gratefully ackowledged: Learning Styles Model by Dr. Rita Dunn and Dr. Kenneth Dunn; 4MAT Model by Dr. Bernice McCarthy, from *The 4MAT System: Teaching to Learning Styles with Right/Left Mode Techniques* (Excel,Inc.); quotations from *Multiple Intelligences: The Theory in Practice* by Howard Gardner (HarperCollins Publishers); *A Celebration of Intelligences,* words by Sonja Walker; photographs pages 19 and 87 by Jim Selby; drawings on pages 49, 76, 79 by Emily Taylor; Peanut People illustrations on p. 97 by Isabel Esterman.

Book and cover design by M.M. Esterman

Cover painting by Periklis Pagratis

For information contact:

> Great Ocean Publishers
> 294 Lone Pine Road
> Alexander, NC 28701-9714

Library of Congress Cataloging in Publication Data

Ellison, Launa, 1944 -

Seeing with magic glasses : a teacher's view from the front line of the learning revolution / Launa Ellison.
Includes bibliographical references and index.
ISBN 0-915556-22-7

1. Learning, Psychology of. 2. Elementary school teaching — Minnesota — Case studies. 3. Ellison, Launa, 1944 - 4. Teachers — Minnesota — Biography. 5. Cognition in children — Minnesota. 6. Educational change — Minnesota. I. Title

LB1060.E45   1993

370.15'23—dc20   93-29173

Printed in the United States of America

Contents

Seeing With Magic Glasses

This story takes place in a public elementary school in the city of Minneapolis. It is a true story. It is my classroom.

I began my teaching career in a suburb in 1964. I knew little about children or the brain's role in learning. The concept of quality education then was vastly different from my vision of excellence today.

I write this story as a teacher. But it would be more appropriate to say the children, the eight hundred children who have passed through my life, were my teachers. I have learned patience and wonder from first graders. I have learned humor and wisdom from eighth graders. I have grown in understanding.

My classroom is in an old building on a half city block. Here I have taught first through eighth graders. My story focuses on the past two years when I have taught fifth through seventh graders and fourth to sixth graders. I invite you to join us in your imagination as I describe our reality. I encourage you to come and learn with us. I invite you into our lives.

Imagine a classroom without assigned seats, where children use the space cooperatively. Imagine healthy green plants lining the large southern windows and topping off the five foot high bookcase full of children's books. Imagine the classroom space separated into smaller areas by burlapped dividers covered with children's art.

As you enter, notice a larger space comprising a fourth of the classroom. This area is our community gathering place; it is a listening and planning place. It also serves as a group teaching area with chalkboards, film screen and video access. A small couch and floor pillows add comfort here. Maps and globes are handy for immediate reference during discussions.

My desk in the opposite corner is almost hidden by my overflowing storage closet, whose shelves are lined with items I need quickly or often — poetry books, colored pencils and art supplies, including many sizes of paper, read-aloud books, marked up copies of novels for group projects, math manipulatives, magnets, tin foil, sandwich bags and a hundred other things.

Near the doorway of our old-fashioned coat hall another cabinet contains shelves of games and daily art supplies. Encyclopedias, almanacs, dictionaries and thesauruses fill reference shelves. A large four-drawer file cabinet houses my students' portfolios of their special work. Children's personal supplies are contained within tattered rubber washtubs on assorted shelves around the room.

In your imagination see the children, a tapestry of sizes, shapes and colors busily engaged in a wide assortment of activities — some working on a computer simulation, others working on a creative play about a novel they just read. Some children are doing math pages, while others are stringing Ojibwa Dream Catchers. Hear them asking questions and giving advice to one another. Hear the natural sounds of children helping children. Sense the happy, relaxed atmosphere, the calm amidst the activity, as students move freely in our space to learn. A sense of caring permeates the space, caring about each other and caring about learning.

These are all things which I hope a visitor to my classroom will observe, as I hope that readers will be able to see them in their mind's eye. But there is something more to be seen, something more vivid, exciting, and inspiring: the wonderful uniqueness and potential of each and every child in the room. This, I believe, is the sight that brings most teachers to the classroom in the first place, and which inspires their best efforts and their commitment to their calling.

In recent years, we have learned a great deal about the mysteries of the brain, about how learning occurs. These insights have formed the basis of a revolution in classroom teaching and learning, a revolution which is still in progress, and which has yet to reach many schools.

It has been my experience that teachers who use these new insights wisely have gained a new perspective, a set of magic glasses, which enables them to see and understand their students and their particular needs as learners, to perceive and nurture the individuality and promise of all their children.

I'd like you to see my children, all our children, through these magic glasses. Join us as we start the school year. Live with us as we grow and learn.

Starting Out:
The Crucial First Week

Coming to now ... The first hour ... Relax and breathe ... Fight or flight ... Belonging ...
Emotions ... Cooperative TEAM's ... Auditory, visual, tactile/kinesthetic strategies ...
Teaching social skills ... Mistake-making ... Review.

Coming to now . . . my hopes and dreams for this year

I am a teacher, I love my work. Educating, captivating the minds of young people, fills me with a sense of grand purpose. Every day is different. My students intrigue and delight me as their knowledge grows, as their ideas germinate. I have not always been as successful as I am now. Though never lacking in will, earlier in my career I did lack the preparation to really be successful. I was a little blind. I did not understand that different students need different treatment to really flourish in school. I should have known better because I myself had suffered the effects of insensitive, roughshod schooling.

When I was five I fell in love with school. My older sister had already begun. She was so lucky to leave each morning on the school bus. She was so grown up.

I had begun to read and I dearly wanted to go to that magical place called "school." But that school, in 1950, had no kindergarten. I must have pleaded relentlessly because eventually my mother asked the school to "test" me for early entrance into first grade.

I passed the test!

I began school! My life was exciting, joyful, complete.

The year progressed and I was successful. I was learning. Then my father was transferred to another town. I left my supportive community and my beloved school. I had to readjust my life to a new school, in a larger city.

So I began school again. But this time the school was not a supportive, caring community.

The blank margins are space for your thoughts, and action plans. I encourage you to write reflections as you read, to capture your reactions and explore your feelings.

Everything was strange and confusing. As my mother tells it, my new teacher was lifeless, burned-out and looking forward to retirement. She was also nearly deaf. She yelled. Maybe she yelled because she couldn't hear herself. Maybe she yelled because her life hadn't turned out the way she had hoped. All I know is she yelled.

She scared me.

I froze.

I went to school everyday. I attended class. But, I didn't learn. Mother was repeatedly told that I was "slow," significantly behind. Yet, she believed in me. She pleaded, "Just leave her alone, give her time. She'll be all right." My mother knew my true potential — a potential that had been ignited then snuffed out.

I reached fifth grade without significant improvement in my reading or other academic skills. Mrs. Zimmerman was my teacher. She was older, experienced. Somehow I began to learn. Even more importantly the next year she taught 6th grade and I was able to remain in her care. After years of drought I began to learn, but my low self-esteem followed me throughout the rest of my formal education, all the way through college.

I had been teaching elementary school for six years when my husband and I adopted a 5 month old boy. I felt confident about his learning. I knew how to teach. I knew what the "experts" said about how to prepare little ones for a successful school experience — read to your child often, encourage your child to draw and color — that would ensure the child's success.

Wrong.

I had been entrusted with this child's life. I had accepted this responsibility willingly. But the "expert advice" didn't work. My son would not sit still. Reading, drawing, and coloring did not interest him.

Intuitively I knew that "forcing" my son was not the answer. Somehow there was something the "experts" were missing. It was years before I understood what that "something" was.

Fifteen years ago, spurred on by another parent's crisis with her brain-injured child, my school applied for and received a grant to study "whole-brain" education and learning styles. Over a three year period we, the staff and parents, studied and shared every bit of information we could find. I began to understand my personal educational struggle, and

I finally had words and systems to explain my son's experience.

I had spent years of schooling in a "fight or flight" stage, frozen in fear. In addition, I realized that I am a visual and kinesthetic learner. School lessons had been primarily taught through lecturing, and I did not learn well through my ears.

My son has always been highly kinesthetic — a whole-body learner. The school system had not known how to meet his learning needs. As a strong Sensor he needed to have his whole body involved to internalize meaning. As an Introverted Feeler he kept his emotions deep inside, never complaining of his treatment in classes.

When I began to understand the implications of learning styles, and how the brain responds to fear, my teaching career was energized with excitement. It was no longer necessary for a child to be the one "right kind" of learner. Now there were systems which allowed me, a teacher, to understand the educational needs of all learners and thus foster their success.

These systems were like magic glasses. They gave me penetrating eyes to "see" each child more fully. Suddenly, I had words, concepts to help me describe their unique learning characteristics and help me guide their experiences.

Today I await my new class of students filled with joyful anticipation of their success. My classroom is a success classroom; every child learns. I am a teacher for all children, each child. The better I learn each child's needs, the better I am able to educate each child.

Tomorrow a new school year will begin. I am excited to begin again the intriguing, magical process that helps me discover the keys for success for these children.

∞

The first day of school ... anxiety marks this day, a day with the potential for positive beginnings or impending disaster. Children enter nervously, parents "drop" their child at the door, peering in with caution. "It's OK" I smile, "I believe in your child. We'll be all right together." The first day of the school year is pregnant with hopes and fears.

As children enter, I greet them and explain their first assignment: "Five tasks are posted around the room. Please do them all in the next few minutes." The tasks help orient them to the room ... "Erase your name from the chalkboard showing you have arrived . . . Label your coat hook with this large silver sticker . . . Staple together a journal and put your name on the front in a design . . . Choose an interesting book . . . Find a comfortable spot to sit down and begin reading." The numbered task cards are purposefully spread around the room enabling students to explore our learning environment.

When the last of the stragglers have had enough time to settle in, I call the group together. "Show me with your fingers, on a scale of 0 to 5, 5 being the most, how nervous are you this morning." The hands go up slowly, some more honest than others, but that will come. In time, in each child's own time, he or she will begin to trust, trust other children enough to respond immediately and honestly, trust me and most importantly trust their own internal understandings. This is the important first, the first time of the first day of a new opportunity to learn more about themselves. I want them to begin. I want them to begin learning to understand who they really are.

"Relax and breathe," I say. They look at me with strange disbelief. Breathe? Of course we're breathing, or we'd be dead. What is she talking about? Without delay I assure them that I know they are breathing but want them to learn to breathe all the way to their brains. "Your brains need one fifth of all of your oxygen and food energy to function well. So you need to breathe deeply expanding your stomachs fully." (Footnotes will give you additional sources of information on the topic.)

We practice breathing. Some children are serious, some are silly. I'm walking the fine line of trust and control. It is a daily line if I'm going to stretch each child to his or her greatest potential. I walk near those who are uncomfortably silly, assuring them I am serious. "This is an important skill, a lifelong skill. Learn to give your body what it needs to do your work. This is a basic health skill, and I do want you to be healthy!" It is the first of many times I need to reassure the children that I want them to be OK. "I want each of you to do your best, to always be your best. I believe in you. I value you." So we learn to breathe. We begin to learn how to choose to relax.

Each day some precious minutes are used to build students' skills of deliberate relaxation. I demonstrate progressive relaxation as I squinch and squeeze my face into tense contortions, entertaining my students a bit, then I relax. I tighten my shoulders, my arms. I make a fist and

"Treat people as if they were what they ought to be and you help them become what they're capable of being"

— *Goethe*

squeeze, squeeze, squeeze then relax. I continue down my body. I ask the children to follow along. We tighten and relax all the way to our toes. Tightening and relaxing help my novices understand the feeling of tension in their bodies.[1] When they have learned deliberate relaxation, I will be able to ask them to think about their bodies, gently identifying any tension and releasing it. Relaxation will become a normal routine.

I have a more selfish reason for teaching my students to relax. Once they've learned to release their tension, I have an effective discipline technique. As the class becomes a bit too loud, a bit too squirrelish or unfocused, I simply spend a few minutes talking them through a relaxation.[2] I help them refocus their energy in a positive way. Relaxation is a gentler, more productive method to control the energies of 30 children than raising my voice in frustration.

The biological processes of breathing and relaxation relate to focusing attention. Brain researchers now understand the dynamics of "attending." The oldest part of our brains, the Reptilian brain, monitors relaxation and stress. An inch of structures at the top of our spinal cord is responsible for routine body functions such as breathing, blood pressure, energy peak time of day, and hunger.[3] Within it the Reticular Activating System (RAS) acts as the brain's chief dispatcher. Each moment the RAS receives thousands of messages — the body's temperature, a sore toe, the binding of clothing, the teacher's voice. The RAS sorts these messages and determines what to send on to "conscious thought". Relaxation impacts the RAS as it sorts messages. Deliberate relaxation can significantly affect our body systems. Blood pressure can be controlled with relaxation. The immune system is affected by relaxation or stress. Relaxing reduces stress and helps the RAS consciously focus our attention. Relaxation is a skill that will benefit my students their whole lives.

The Reptilian brain also controls our "fight or flight" response. Should we stay and fight, or run away to safety? Chemicals in the brain respond whenever we are physically or emotionally threatened. Many people have heard about adrenaline's incredible surge under stress, but other chemicals, such as catecholamines and cortisol, also pop into the bloodstream.[4] These "fight or flight" chemicals are important in stimulating a quick response. However, living with a continual level of stress damages the delicate workings of our bodies over time.[5] Relaxation

"Every second 100 million messages from our nervous system bombard our brain. Only several hundred are permitted above our brainstem, and only a few of these receive some sort of response."
— *Jack Maguire, Care and Feeding of the Brain*

clears these chemicals and promotes health.

The children in my care will think better, learn more, and be healthier without significant stress in the classroom. But does that mean schoolwork should be easy? Absolutely not! It does means that work should be "hard enough but not too hard." It means a math assignment is neither too hard, nor is it already known. It means that if a student receives 100% on a spelling pretest, there's an alternative assignment ready to learn. I don't want any students bored, wasting their time, or stuck, wasting their time. Each student's task must be just challenging enough, a gentle stretch within reach.

Our first day continues with a change of pace and purposeful socializing. "Boys and girls, as you get up from the meeting take a 'People Hunt' from the counter. You will have 15 minutes to move around the room and get other student's names for each description. For example, number 5, does anyone have initials which spell a word?"

This activity looks simple enough but its purpose is deep. I'm placating the old Reptilian, need-for-safety brain. Once a room full of strangers become known quantities the classroom feels safer and the RAS will turn its attention to academic learning rather than focusing on the newness. The People Hunt is not frivolous. It is brain-wise. We can't circumvent how our brains work. If I don't take the time to build a safe community, the RAS will continue tuning into the potential threat of strangers in our close encounters.

Abraham Maslow identified a hierarchy of human needs long before the Reptilian brain was understood. Physiological needs are the first level; safety needs are level two; belonging is the third level. Knowing each others' names is part of making the classroom a safe, belonging place. When needs at these levels are thwarted, it is more difficult for the brain to focus on learning academic skills.

I assign a second "belonging" activity on the first day: a personal collage. This activity can be as complicated as explaining a European coat of arms or Native American shield, or simply "with words and pictures fill this page with ideas that show what you like, who you are. We'll decorate this bulletin board with your personal collages." My purpose is to immediately acknowledge each child's visibility in our room. Being visible is important. An artistic expression of one's self promotes a sense of "I belong here." (Please note the use of "arts"

"Making maximum connections in the brain requires a state we describe as 'relaxed alertness'. This is a combination of low threat and high challenge."

— *Caine and Caine*

"In general, only a child who feels safe dares to grow forward healthily. His safety needs must be gratified. He can't be pushed ahead, because the ungratified safety needs will forever remain underground, always calling for satisfaction."

— *Abraham Maslow*

activities throughout my curriculum. Art is a vehicle for communication. Art skills are developed through specific lessons and then used for the expression of ideas in all curriculum areas.)

The RAS constantly interacts with the next brain level which deals with emotions. In order to free my students attention for optimal learning I must create a calm emotional environment.

Emotions are the domain of the Limbic System, the middle brain system consisting of two inches of structures wrapped around the Reptilian brain.[7] It includes the pituitary, thalamus, hypothalamus, hippocampus and amygdala. The entire area is rich in chemical messengers, called neurotransmitters, which are the biological equivalents of joy, pleasure, fear, anger, and aggression. The hippocampus and amygdala play important roles in memory.

Some of these chemicals, endorphins (*endo*genous m*orphins* = morphins produced within), serve as the body's natural opium. They create the natural highs — an anticipation of seeing your lover, the exhilaration of "runner's high", and the inner joy of a significant accomplishment. One endorphin is associated with a sense of calm; another endorphin creates a sense of pleasure.[8]

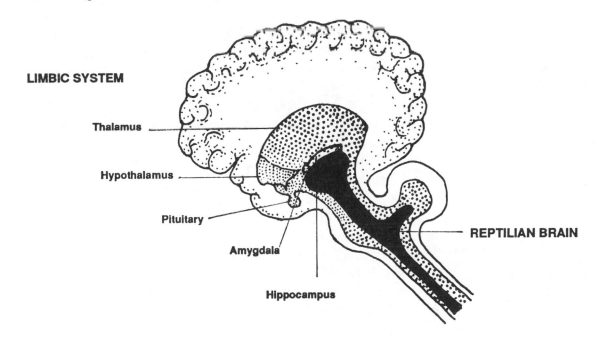

LIMBIC SYSTEM

Thalamus

Hypothalamus

Pituitary

Amygdala

Hippocampus

REPTILIAN BRAIN

Neurotransmitters are also chemically linked to our negative states. Substance P sounds the "pain" alarm. Too little norepinephrine results in depression. Neurotransmitters have been linked to a wide variety of disorders from schizophrenia to Sudden Infant Death Syndrome.

Within the Limbic System the pea-sized master gland, the hypothalamus, gives directions to the pituitary, which in turn gives directions to bones, the thyroid, and sex organs. The hypothalamus exerts tremendous power over our lives. It receives **all internal** sensory messages alerting us to feelings of hunger, thirst, and exhaustion. It regulates body temperature, blood pressure and sleep. On the other hand, the thalamus receives **all external** sensory information, information from outside the body, except smell. Smells reach the cerebral cortex directly and may be the most powerful sensory memory.

Messages from our nervous system, our endocrine system, and our sensory systems are processed first by the Reptilian system, then the emotional Limbic system. Schools have ignored, or been unaware of, the processes of these two brain systems when they expect students to simply "think" with their cerebral cortex. It can't be done. Humans are whole-brained. The whole brain works together all of the time. Thus, just as teachers expect children to follow the rules, it's time educators follow the rules of the human brain. Teachers must address safety issues, body comfort issues, and emotional issues. When these issues are dealt with appropriately the brain will have enough focused attention left over for "school thinking".

A cooperative, collegial classroom respects both the Limbic and Reptilian systems. Bell curve classrooms are designed so there are only a few winners. Beating others in order to be best stimulates the Reptilian and Limbic systems to be on guard. It ties up the brain's energy in a fight or flight syndrome: "Will I make it or shall I just give up?" A competitive system promotes the flight of students who give up and drop out of school.

Why not have competition? Competition "causes anxiety . . . is inefficient . . . undermines intrinsic motivation . . . destroys self-esteem . . . poisons relationships."
— *Alfie Kohn, No Contest: The Case Against Competition*

In my classroom cooperative groups facilitate a respect for all learners. "I believe you are all winners. And I believe you have different strengths. I want you to learn to use each other's strengths to learn more, faster." I pass out TEAM cards randomly. Later in the year when I know children's strengths and needs I may deliberately compose cooperative groups. Now random groups are effective. TEAM cards are created simply by writing a T, E, A or M on a 3 x 5 index card, using a different color marker for each set of letters. As I pass out the cards I ask the children to find others with their TEAM colors. Thirty students are organized into 8 groups in a matter of minutes.

Each of the TEAM letters represent a responsibility in the small group. With a colorful poster in hand, I explain the responsibilities behind each letter. "T stands for the Task clarifier. T's please stand. Your job is to be sure you understand what the group is to accomplish and help keep your group on task and working toward your goal. Would one of the T's restate, what is your job?"

What have I done? I've used the poster for visual learners. I've asked the T's to stand, signaling their importance. I've involved physical movement for the tactile/kinesthetic learners. I've explained verbally for the auditory learners and I've checked for understanding, reinforcing the information. As the student restates, I point to the relevant information on the chart, nodding my affirmation and thanking the student for good listening. This took only minutes but it's thoroughly planned to engage all students' learning modalities.

I continue explaining the TEAM symbols and their tasks. The E, signifying the Encourager, is responsible for group support, keeping everyone involved and rewarded with encouraging comments. I ask the children to share their experience of being in groups where everyone did not cooperate. Children respond: "I didn't like it. I got stuck with all the work." "I felt left out." "I got angry!" I restate my expectation that group work means everyone is involved. Involvement doesn't mean everyone does the same thing, rather it means a commitment to be actively contributing. It means sharing ideas and skills.

A is the Articulator. This person's task is to keep the records and report back to the class. This task may be difficult for a randomly assigned student. Any task may seem difficult to a particular individual but all tasks are supported by the TEAM as a whole. If an individual has difficulty spelling, other team members are expected to help spell but not write it for her. If a student is nervous giving a report to the whole class, the small group can have him practice with them before he speaks to the larger group.

The student with the M card is the Mover. She is the only group member who should be out of her seat. In today's activity the Mover will need to get paper for the group. In a science activity Movers get and return all of the equipment. The Mover also finds me if the group needs help to continue successfully.

"Your first task is to teach each other your first name and how to spell it. Some of you are auditory learners. Auditory learners will be able to remember how to spell the names by hearing the letters. Some of you are visual learners. Visual means seeing. What do you suppose is a good way for you to learn spelling? Yes, writing it down . . . Using bright markers . . . Seeing each letter in your imagination. Those are all good methods for visual learners. Some of you are tactile/kinesthetic learners. This means you learn best when you touch or when your whole body is involved. How can the tactile (touch)/kinesthetic (whole body movement) learners practice spelling your names? Try writing it in the air using your whole arm or with a wet paint brush on the chalkboard."[9]

"As you are learning each others' names, experiment with the auditory, visual and tactile/kinesthetic ways of learning. You are all different. You'll learn more easily and quickly if you figure out the way your brain prefers to learn. Discuss how the different methods feel for you." As groups learn each other's names, I give them a list of all thirty student names. I ask them to connect names with faces and learn the spellings. By expecting students to learn each person's name I validate each student's importance in our class.

The small groups begin working. I move through the room quietly listening, showing approval of good group work processes or asking who is playing a role, if the role isn't obvious. This also gives me the opportunity to have personal eye contact with every student. It is important that each of my students feel visible, and connect with me, on this first day of school.

Why are cooperative groups important? Significant research indicates that cooperative groups break down traditional boundaries.[10] On this first day I am setting the expectation that we will be a cooperating community. I expect students to work together across the traditional boundaries of friendship, race, socioeconomics and gender. I've begun the process to eliminate status ordering which sets up the "smart" to receive glory and the "dumb" to withdraw. I've also begun to explain different learning styles. No one's learning style is better or worse. They are just different. I've asked students to experience different ways of

learning and to think about what works for them. Group roles have established each student's importance. Each individual, by doing his own task, supports his groups' success. The group work is completed when every member is successful. Everyone masters the task. Cooperative group work is active learning, sharing, listening, talking, doing. It engages more thinking than passive lectures. All students are able to learn more with cooperation.[11]

Cooperation is a crucial skill in our adult world. It has the potential of impacting issues in the global village by defusing the international struggle for dominance. The learning of cooperative behaviors begins within each individual and requires time to be established as habit. Over the year my students will become more skilled in cooperative groups. Their self understandings and interpersonal skills will become more refined. To set this potential in motion I use cooperative group work on the first day.

Appropriate social skills are learned behaviors. In past years many social skills were learned at home. In today's world I do not assume students have internalized appropriate social skills. I teach social skills directly, beginning the first day. Years ago our school adopted seven positive behavior expectations. These expectations include:

In our school "great emphasis was placed on our learning to work with others — to use our individual talents in such a way that we could enrich each other's experiences. We felt that it was just as important to learn to appreciate and respect each other; to live sensitively and compassionately and to take responsibility for our own behavior as it was to learn the multiplication tables or to memorize the capitals of each state."

— *Eda LeShan*

Do your best work always[12]

Use your best judgment when making choices

Use your time wisely: stay on task

Be prepared for learning with the proper materials

Respect school and personal property

Listen to, learn from and be courteous to others

Respect the rights of others: be verbally and physically considerate.[13]

Seven red and white banners, one for each expectation, hang in our school's main hall; brightly colored posters are visible in every classroom.

During this first week I introduce all the expectations. Then I develop one expectation each week. I use many techniques to help students internalize these expectations. We discuss "When did you do your best work? How do you know it was your best?" A parent and I model courteous interpersonal problem-solving. Students create plays showing positive behaviors rather than the negative alternatives.

I also give out SCAMO[14] tickets to reinforce students' positive behaviors. Giving tickets for Showing Caring About Myself and Others is a "catch them being good" technique. When the week's emphasis is "Use your time wisely," I watch for students concentrating well and slip a ticket into their hands while verbally reinforcing "Good use of your time."

The student puts his name on the ticket and puts it in the SCAMO container, which means a chance for prizes. The prizes may be a pencil, a notebook, other school supplies or an item donated by local merchants. Students look forward to the SCAMO drawings. The actual drawing is done privately, usually random, but sometimes to reinforce a particular student I search for a ticket with the right name. I keep a record of SCAMO winners, striving for race and gender equity.

Teaching prosocial skills is an important, long-term commitment which I begin on the first day of school. Appropriate social skills are a key element in drug prevention programs like the Lions Clubs International's *Skills for Adolescence, Skills for Growing*[15] and police departments' DARE program.[16]

> "A successful school is a cohesive community of shared values, beliefs, rituals and ceremonies."
>
> *— Brendtro, Brokenleg, Brockern*

∞

Mistake making is an important learning process. I want my students to learn "how to learn" from their mistakes rather than hide mistakes or let mistakes block them. Thomas Edison wasn't limited by his mistakes. He replied to a frustrated worker, "We've made a lot of progress. At least we know 8,000 things that won't work."

Last year I began violin lessons. I practiced so hard. I, a capable adult, did not want to look incompetent when I played my weekly piece. After much time and stress, I realized I was defeating my own joy of playing. I am not perfect. My violin teacher needs to hear my mistakes to understand how to help me.

When a student does everything right in my classroom I have to teach without important clues. Student "mistakes" give me the opportunity to reflect on the student's thinking, thus enabling me to understand where I need to develop a concept more fully.

My task, this first week of school, is to begin to convince students that it is OK, even important, to make mistakes. It's important to ask questions. If a student doesn't ask questions when he needs to, he robs himself. If students mask their mistakes by having parents or friends do their homework or don't have "permission" to ask questions, I don't have the information I need.

Making mistakes is OK in our room, but its often a foreign idea to students. I must be aware of my reaction to my mistakes and to students' mistakes. Instead of stating directly that Johnny has made a mistake I phrase it in softer words, "Johnny, did you goof? Do you want to think about it again or may I help you?" For my own many mistakes I have a standard line, "That's my first mistake this year!" Of course my students see the humor and enjoy my line. It relieves the heaviness of expecting themselves to be perfect.

Student mistakes on pre-tests are an important way for me to understand skill levels. Some students, however, think a test is a test. I reassure them that pre-tests are for me the teacher. Accurate pre-tests give me crucial information about my student needs. I explain to students that pre-tests are for my benefit; pre-tests help me understand what to teach. This week I begin to have my students take pre-tests in math and spelling.

What are my goals this first week? They include encouraging students to believe in themselves, and begin to trust me. I focus on activities to provide for comfort, safety and belonging. I invite students to learn how they best learn. I emphasize my belief that all students are different and all are valuable.[17] I put everyone's work on our bulletin boards. I invite everyone to achieve rather than honoring only "the best." I set the expectation that cooperation, helping others learn, will be the norm. I begin the process of helping students understand the growth opportunity in mistakes. I begin teaching social skills. My words and my actions are designed to speak clearly, "I invite you to grow, I believe in you. I want you to learn."

-∞-

[1] These responses are documented in James Humphreys book, *Teaching Children to Relax* (Charles Thomas Publishing: 1988).
[2] For 35 creative relaxation scripts, suitable for K-8 read Martha Belknap, *Taming Your Dragons* (D.O.K. Publishers: 1990), or *A Peaceable Classroom* by Harmin and Sax (Winston Press: 1974).

[3] For more detailed information of the Reptilian system read Bloom, Lazerson and Hofstadter, *Brain, Mind and Behavior* (Educational Broadcasting Corp: 1985).

[4] *Ibid.*

[5] Herbert Benson, *The Relaxation Response* (William Morrow Co.: 1975).

[6] You can make up your own or use "Making New Friends," a reproducible activity page published in the September issue of *Learning 88*.

[7] Bloom, *Brain, Mind and Behavior.*

[8] Deva and James Beck, *The Pleasure Connection: How Endorphins Affect Our Health and Happiness* (Synthesis Press: 1987).

[9] I will develop learning modalities in greater detail in the chapter on learning styles. A good place to start understanding more is Walter Barbe's, *Growing Up Learning* (Acropolis Books: 1985).

[10] Robert Slavin, *Cooperative Learning* (Longman Publishing: 1983).

[11] Resources for further information include Phi Delta Kappa's 90 cents fastback, *Cooperative Learning*, Elizabeth Cohen's *Designing Groupwork* (Teachers College Press: 1986) or numerous books and videos by Johnson and Johnson, available through Interaction Books, 7208 Cornelia Drive, Edina MN 55435.

[12] For more discussion on "doing your best" read William Glasser's *The Quality School* (Harper and Row: 1990).

[13] Good reproducible conflict resolution lessons are found in Fran Schmidt and Alice Friedman's *Creative Conflict Solving for Kids.* (Grace Contrino Adams Peace Education Foundation: 1986) P.O. Box 19-1153, Miami Beach, FL 33139.

[14] SCAMO is taken from Ellen McGinnis and Arnold Goldstein, *Skillstreaming the Elementary School Child.* (Research Press Co.: 1984), p.60.

[15] For further information on the Quest programs, training and materials, call 800-446-2700.

[16] An international program, DARE began in Los Angeles. Their phone is 800-223-DARE.

[17] For more ideas about inviting students to learn read William Purkey and John Novak's *Inviting School Success* (Wadsworth Publishing: 1987), or John Wilson's *The Invitational Elementary Classroom* (Charles Thomas Publishing: 1986).

A Multicultural Interdisciplinary Theme: People

Personal questions ... Connecting to ... Webbing ME stories ... Personal timelines ...
Introducing learning styles ... Racial understanding ... Graphing data ... Presentations ...
Family heritages ... Global studies ... Media and lifestyles ... Positive role models ... Reports ...
Make and do ... The human body ... Accomplishments.

A People Theme is our first course of study. I begin with this because it is personal. It focuses on students' interests, their families and their bodies. It includes the broader issues of race, lifestyle, and the significant contributions of people. The People theme is an interdisciplinary study, spanning different subjects. It interacts with the particular interests and needs of my students and is deeply rooted within the school district's curriculum objectives. This People theme is also an appropriate sub-theme within our school's chosen focus for the year.

Each spring my school chooses one broad theme for the following school year. This year our general theme of "Changes, Choices, Challenges" focuses on decision-making and the changes that occur in all people's lives. Other recent themes have been "Bridges to Awareness" and "Dream Seekers, Earth Keepers"[1] which focused on personal dreams of quality lives and our environmental responsibilities.

To prepare for our school-wide theme a committee brainstorms (webs) all possible concepts and connections. We identify the important core concepts. For example, the People theme encompasses concepts of race, lifestyle, famous people's contributions, as well as family background, the physical body and feelings. Teachers gather a wide variety of resources (rather than using a textbook) and share ideas with each other. Each theme meets the needs of our kindergarten to eighth grade students, yet adapts to the differing requirements of particular classrooms. The school-wide theme connects knowledge and skill within our children's minds and connects all children in our school within our thematic activities. The theme appears and reappears on our bulletin boards, in our school's weekly news home, and in our assembly programs.

Thematic teaching is a more brain-friendly approach than the usual method of classroom presentation that separates subjects into discreet, unconnected areas. Our thematic curriculum purposefully makes connections. By linking many content areas, we construct higher level concepts that help us understand the patterns, meaning and utility of the information we study. Thematic teaching also allows us to practice and apply basic math and language skills within a rich, and relevant context connecting children's lives with science and social studies concepts.

"Fertile themes for integrative learning are like . . . a good lens. A good lens . . . applies broadly. A good lens . . . applies pervasively. A good lens . . . discloses fundamental patterns. A good lens . . . reveals similarities and contrasts. A good lens . . . fascinates."
— *David Perkins*[2]

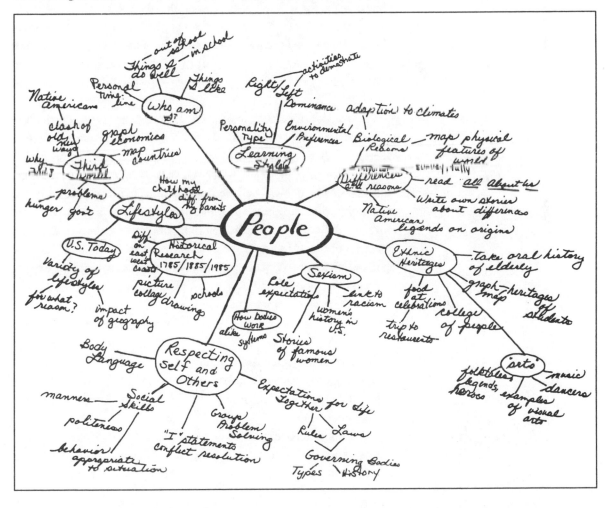

I begin by asking personal questions. "Who are you? What do you like to do? What do you like to learn? Who are the other people in our classroom? What do they care about?" Questions begin an internal process of putting information into meaningful patterns. Questions frame problem-finding, an important step before information seeking.

An essential question[3] in my classroom is "Who are you?" Three reasons make this the appropriate place to start. First, people are basically egocentric: students are intrinsically motivated to participate because they are learning about themselves. The second reason is equally important; my effectiveness as a teacher depends on how well I know my learners. To successfully plan curriculum I must understand who each learner is, what each learner already knows, what she cares about and what her skill level is in each particular area. Finally, I begin with this theme because it is a natural link to multicultural issues. The People Theme creates a natural setting to discuss different skin colors and differing lifestyles. The topic promotes a respectful atmosphere for individual differences.

Many educators recognize the importance of beginning curriculum with what the student is thinking. Madeline Hunter notes that motivation is significantly increased "by utilizing students' interest in themselves."[4] Hunter's first step, the anticipatory set, connects a topic with what the student already knows, believes or feels. This step increases the motivation to learn because it frames the questions in relation to the individual. Bernice McCarthy refers to similar processes in the First Quadrant of the 4MAT System[5]. Activities in the first quadrant draw upon the students experiences, discussing and relating previous experiences to a new topic.

Connecting to prior knowledge is critical for the brain. When we connect previous understandings to new learning we give the brain a hook, and the brain organizes the new concepts with the old. Often teachers spend inadequate time setting up such connections for students. By ignoring this basic need and rushing into the content, teachers defeat their own purpose — student learning. For success, we must teach the way the brain learns.

Writing about oneself is inherently interesting to students. I use this writing assignment to teach webbing,[6] also known as mind mapping,[7] and topic sentences. I demonstrate webbing on the chalkboard, by putting my name in a circle and asking, "How would you describe me?" Students usually suggest physical descriptions first; I put a line outward from the circle clustering the descriptions around the word "physical". Beyond that I probe, "What do you think I like?" Another line is drawn out from the hub with the label "likes". The children suggest subtopics which include food and hobbies, as I model connecting thoughts to a label. I continue with spokes relating to my "job" and "family".

I have modelled this webbing process. Now I ask students to put the word "ME" (or their name) in the center of their blank page and the subtopics "physical", "likes", "school" since that is their job, and "family". They randomly jot down the ideas which pop into their minds. I watch and encourage, allowing enough time for everyone to successfully fill his page with ideas. Encouragingly I explain, "The more descriptors the better."

"Now you are going to use your descriptors to write an essay about yourself. Decide which of your ideas will be first. Label that group #1 and continue numbering all of your groups." Then, modelling with a student example, I write a topic sentence on the chalkboard. The sentence tells what the paragraph is about without giving significant information. For example: *There are many activities I like to do in my spare time. Three people live in my house.* I help individual students create topic sentences for their groups of linked ideas. When students begin to write, they begin with their topic sentences and continue with the supporting details in their webs. This structure allows students to organize their ideas effectively.

Each "ME" story is wonderfully unique and clear. Students feel successful. I want them to be successful in each educational experience, to benefit from the rush of endorphins (a natural brain chemical associated with pleasurable experiences) that accompanies feelings of accomplishment. The stronger a pleasant memory, the more likely the child will want to repeat the experience.[8] Endorphins rewarding success is the biological basis of the old adage, "Nothing breeds success like success!"

Webbing, the process of brainstorming in any order then organizing the information, is a whole-brain technique allowing a random flow of ideas (simultaneous, right-hemisphere activity) before evaluating and sequencing the thoughts (critical, left-hemisphere activity). Webbing before any writing increases student success.

Adults in our school have chosen to use our first names with students. We believe respect is built on a relationship, not on the use of titles.

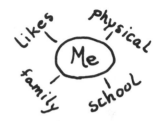

As part of the People Theme we create personal timelines. This is an integrating activity connecting my students' pasts to their present experience. "Today's homework is special," I begin. "You are to talk to an adult in your family about your life. Find out when you learned to walk, to talk, and other things that have happened in your life. Find photographs, drawings, clothes or items from your past." (Caution: I try to be sensitive for the child who may not have a personal history in saved pictures and memorabilia. I encourage her to draw pictures from the personal oral history shared by a relative.)

This gathering of information takes time, so I assign this task days before I plan to begin. In the interim I show examples of timelines emphasizing the consistent space between demarcations.

Days pass and my students have collected the "stuff" of their lives. Brown paper bags, overflowing with the stuff, line our classroom. "The first step is to lay out your stuff in a line, putting pictures and memorabilia in time order. What is the root word of 'memorabilia'? Right 'memory', 'memorabilia' is the stuff of memories". I underline the word's root on the chalkboard. "The amount of space your memorabilia takes will determine the length of your timeline. After you lay out your items get a strip of paper that will fit it." I encourage students to work in pairs helping one another to plan. Measuring accurate spacing for each year is the key skill. I watch my students' process, helping as needed, to ensure everyone's success. Each timeline becomes beautifully different, as unique as each student creating it. During our next group meeting students explain their timelines with pride.

Creation of the timelines involved much valuable work. Students were required to synthesize, analyze and evaluate information. I used my students' natural interest in themselves to engage them in high quality thinking. My students were deeply involved; they are proud of their achievement.

Our People Theme refocuses on student learning styles. Understanding your own learning style is an important component of learning how to learn. Understanding others' styles encourages respect for these differences. For instance, individuals can greatly differ in the way they prefer to take in information. "We can perceive, or take in information, with our eyes, our ears, our taste, smell and touch. In school the most important senses are our eyes (visual), ears (auditory), touch (tactile) and whole body (kinesthetic)".

I review what we discussed the first week about learning with our senses and elaborate further. "If you are a visual learner, breaking words into syllables is a good strategy." I model on the chalkboard, using a different color for each syllable. "Another good strategy is to remember the shape of the word." I draw around the shape showing the configuration then ask students to close their eyes and see the word. I ask students to write their own name and draw the configuration. We practice with other words.

For auditory practice I clap syllables, *Learn-ing = clap-clap, au-di-to-ry = clap-clap-clap-clap*. Another good approach is to say the letters aloud so you can hear them. You can make audio tapes of the spelling words, reciting a word, pausing (long enough for the word to be written) then spelling each letter to check and correct.

I illustrate the tactile/kinesthetic approach by making large letters on the chalkboard with water and a brush, and in the air using my whole arm. Tactile/kinesthetic students need large muscle involvement. I ask students to practice the different methods with their spelling partner. I want students to experience all three sensory methods in order to feel which works best.

We explore learning styles by discussing individual preferences, then graphing the class's range of preferences. Self-understanding is the important first step to understanding other people. Abraham Maslow said, learning comes "from within out" and the ultimate questions are "Who am I? What am I (in relation to others)?"[9] Graphing student responses clarifies that other people have different learning styles. It creates a bridge from self-understanding to respecting others' differences.

"Knowledge becomes natural when it is sufficiently connected with what is already known."
— *Caine and Caine*

∞

Understanding racial issues is increasingly important in our world. Students need to understand the reasons for different skin colors. To do this I read explanations about the adaptive value of different physical characteristics.[10] Evolutionary processes created light-skinned people and dark-skinned people according to environmental needs. Other group physical features such as shape of noses are related to similar environmental evolutionary processes.

Understanding the relationship between environment and physical features broadens students' respect for the diversity of humans. I wrap up these understandings by linking students to others in the world. "Using these old *National Geographics*, create a collage of peoples' faces from around the world. Include a photograph of yourself somewhere in the collage."

We work with more math, collecting and graphing data about the class. I organize cooperative TEAM's and remind them of their group roles. "Your task is to gather data about people in our class. First decide what you want to investigate." The discussion begins, "Let's graph hair color!" "I want to graph weights." "No, somebody will get mad if we do that." "How about finding out who has pets!" The discussion goes on. The Encourager works to get everyone's ideas out as the Articulator records the brainstorming. In time the Task clarifier asks how they are going to make a decision. The topic for each group is decided.

Next I ask, "How are you going to collect the data?" "Can you get the information by a show of hands? Do you need to talk individually to people, or shall I print up your questions?" TEAMs discuss again and make another decision.

In a few days all groups have their data. I pose the next question, "How are you going to present the data?" We discuss examples of line graphs, bar graphs, picture graphs and circle graphs. "Each graph must be large enough for everyone to see during a whole class presentation. Use color to make your graph easier to understand. Our visual processing hemisphere tunes into the colors on a graph."

TEAMs organize their data and decide on a graphing method. I circulate, supplying the different materials needed for their creative ideas and encouraging students to think a bit more about this or that.

When all TEAMs have finished, the graphs are presented to the whole class. This is one of many opportunities I create for a group to stand up and present in front of the class. Each time the student presents with a group, when the weight of the presentation isn't just on his back but rather a shared responsibility, it is preparation for the time when he will give a presentation alone. Some teachers expect students to "give a speech in front of the class" without previous supportive experiences. That is similar to expecting a child to walk without first crawling. Teachers must understand and plan for the subskills, the sub-experiences, which are necessary to build toward success.

The whole TEAM is in front of the class. In some groups the Articulator explains, other groups have everyone sharing. The large, visually appealing graphs give interesting data about the class. Students are successful because I have coached and supported each group, just inches at a time. When I use another graphing activity in a month (skills need to be continually recycled) students will need less support.

TEAM evaluation is the last step in this process. Students fill out the form individually then discuss their rankings and feelings with the rest of their group.

Am I proud of our final result?	**1 - 2 - 3 - 4 - 5**
Did others listen to my ideas?	**1 - 2 - 3 - 4 - 5**
Did we work together well?	**1 - 2 - 3 - 4 - 5**
Did I do my best job?	**1 - 2 - 3 - 4 - 5**

Self-evaluation is a thoughtful and continual activity which promotes growth.

∞

Investigating family heritages is an individual assignment during our People Theme. Family tree charts usually assume a two parent family. I do not. Such an assumption leaves some students out in the uncomfortable cold. I want each child actively involved. I model different family styles on the chalkboard illustrating diagrams based on lineage from just one parent, from a guardian and step-parent as well as the traditional biological two-parent system.[11] Single parent families are equally respected in my voice tone. Each family's structure must be respected to foster each child's success. This assignment allow students to trace family lines back as far as possible.

Global Studies is our next investigation. I give TEAMs different tasks using the jigsaw model of cooperative learning (meaning everyone has a piece of the puzzle).[12] Groups are given an atlas of world economic maps and different assignments. One group focuses on annual wages, another on number of flush toilets in homes around the world. One group looks at infant mortality rates. I develop the specific assignments according to the most current information I have found. Each group studies their piece and contributes information to the larger picture. Students' shared ignorance begins to decrease and the world map has taken on increased meaning. Then I reflect the findings back to my students' lives. "Did you realize so many people do not have indoor plumbing?" "Did you realize the United States consumes so much of the world's oil compared to other countries?"

Our evaluation of the role of the media begins in a strange way. While discussing the lack of indoor plumbing in some countries the word "lifestyle" was mentioned. A student linked the word to the "Lifestyles of the Rich and Famous." This led to small groups describing different lifestyles in the United States. Students searched popular magazines for images of different lifestyles, only to find some lifestyles invisible. Other students kept a television log, with the same conclusion. I related their ideas back to the students' personal experiences. "Have you ever felt invisible?" "Is your family's lifestyle visible in the media?" "How do you think the invisible people feel? Why?" My students begin to understand the underlying economics of the "invisible people" in the United States. This includes the homeless, the migrants, the poor of Appalachia, immigrants, Hispanic and Native Americans. "What sources of information can we find? Are these people 'covered' in encyclopedias? Why? Are their issues covered in *Time* Magazine or *Newsweek*?" We find statistics on the large numbers of people involved, but little other coverage.

This sequence of lessons is very different from lecturing about the world's inequities. First, I linked students' skin color and physical characteristics with people across the world. Then I linked students' family, ethnic heritages, and the world. Finally, I set up a TEAM investigation of new information, with each group researching and presenting part of the world economic picture. Students made comparisons between their own lives and others' lives across the world.

-∞-

We take up a study of influential people, the famous and not so famous who have made important contributions to society. Again, I begin with what my students know. "Today, working in pairs of your choice, we're going to have a little contest," I explain, handing each pair a small strip of paper. "You will have three minutes to write down as many famous men as you can. Questions? OK, begin." When time has lapsed the pairs tally their totals. I ask, "How many of those men are people of color." Unfortunately, the number is very small. "Of those men of color, how many are famous for contributions outside sports or entertainment?" Usually my students' knowledge is limited to Martin Luther King, Jesse Jackson and Nelson Mandela.

We repeat the process with women. Students know significantly fewer women, and even fewer women of color outside the sports and entertainment fields. We applaud the students with the greatest numbers. I make a quick graph showing the average numbers: white men, men of color, white women, women of color. Then discuss why the results are skewed. "Are women less capable then men? What are the reasons we know less women?" Numerous speculations about sexism are shared. "Why do we know so few people of color?" My students draw the analogy from sexism to racism.

During the next weeks I share vignettes of famous people,[13] particularly women and people of color. I broaden my students' base of knowledge by reading biographies and showing videos. I include stories of youth who have made a difference in their worlds by fighting crime and saving our environment.[14] Then I ask each student to choose a famous person for a written report and 3-D project. Part of my aim is to provide a wide field of positive role models so I explain, "Athletes and entertainers work hard, but they represent less than 1% of the jobs,[15] and

"A teacher affects eternity; he can never tell where his influence stops."

— *Henry Adams*

are often in the spotlight. For this research project you need to choose someone outside the sports and entertainment worlds who has made a significant contribution to the world." They choose Madame Curie, Mahatma Gandhi, Frederick Douglass, Chief Joseph, Robert Goddard, Susan B. Anthony, Sacagawea, Barbara Jordan and others.

We go to the media center to find books on their topics, and I begin to teach them how to take notes. Over the next ten days I purposefully teach each step necessary for writing a quality report. I check on progress as students sort note cards and write topic sentences. I teach introductory paragraphs, the inclusion of visual material, how to set up a table of contents and a bibliography.

When the written reports are finished, I organize circle groups for peer evaluation of the reports. I ask students to sit in groups of 6-8 and I begin the directions, "You each have your own report. In this process you will have the opportunity to look at three other reports and evaluate how well other students developed their reports. You have the evaluation sheets. Be sure to put your name in the 'Evaluated By' spot. Now pass your report twice to the left. Evaluate that report, giving 0 to 5 points for each of the items listed." I wait until everyone is finished evaluating the first report, then repeat the process by passing reports to the left twice.

This evaluation procedure allows students to learn from each other, and reinforces the qualities of a good report. Students are analyzing how well other students have met the standard. Students with poor judgement skills are obvious because other students react to the inappropriateness of their scoring. When student evaluation is complete, I score each report. My score usually turns out to be similar to the average of the student given scores. I give award certificates made with PrintShop software to students who attain 45 or more of the 50 points available, and to all students who finished their reports on time.

The final piece in our study of famous people is the "Make and Do" project and class presentation. A "Make and Do" is something 3-D which couldn't be included in the paper/pencil report. Students create displays of items symbolic of the person's struggles and accomplishments. They create mobiles, sculptures or skits, complete with props and costumes. The reports and presentation materials are displayed in our hall so other students in our school can profit from our work.

∞

REPORT NAME
_____

CREATED BY
_____

Use 0 to 5 (best) to evaluate
Evaluator's Signature:

_____

Cover -- name, author, neat
    picture, color   _____
Table of contents --
    correct order   _____
Introductory paragraph tells
    how report is organized   _____
Topic Sentences -- introduces
    without giving information   _____
Spelling -- correct, readable   _____
Punctuation, paragraphs --
    correct   _____
Quality of information   _____
Illustrations --
    relevant, interesting   _____
Conclusion -- wraps up
    the topic   _____
Bibliography -- all info.,
    alphabetical   _____

    TOTAL POINTS   _____
(If you are dissatisfied with your score, you may
improve it and be scored again.)

Studying the human body is the last part of our People Theme. It brings the theme full circle, back to the students. First we brainstorm to create a list of body parts. Then we organize the parts into body systems: respiratory, circulatory, excretory, skeletal, muscular, nervous, endocrine, reproductive, digestive and the senses. A lively discussion ensues over placing some parts into systems. "Does the heart just belong in the circulatory system? What about its relationship to the respiratory system? Does the brain belong to more than the nervous system? What about its role in bone growth? Or reproductive cycles? Or muscle memory?" My students conclude, quite appropriately, that there is a great amount of overlap. Our body systems are not distinct; they are intrinsically interrelated.

Students list their 1st, 2nd and 3rd choice for studying a body system. I create study TEAMs of three students to research each topic, including a separate brain study group. I balance the groups heterogeneously making sure male/female, minority/majority and all skill levels are represented. "Your first group task is to list three essential questions you want to answer." These questions form the core of the group's study, but do not limit their research.

I explain my expectation for their final result. "Each group is to teach the rest of the class about their body system's functions. Topic sentences should represent the essential learnings to be shared. The presentation must be visual, as well as auditory, and interactive with the class. Each group is to start with a pretest, teach and then post-test. Groups are responsible, not only for presenting information, but for checking to see if other students have learned what they intended to teach."

Some groups create 3-D objects — an old hose tied and coiled representing intestines and a fine sponge representing lungs. Other groups engage students in demonstrations — squeezing our fists 70 times in a minute to represent our heartbeat, optical illusions which demonstrate our eyes' perceptions, a blender demonstration to show the breakdown of food in our stomachs and then squeezing the resulting mush through a cheesecloth to represent the action of the walls of our stomach. The reproductive group creates a lively game show with their information.

Groups show a sense of pride as their post-tests confirm they have really taught others. I have "covered the curriculum" without "teaching". My students actively sought information, evaluated, organized, and transformed it from book reading to interesting presentations.

What did the "People Theme" accomplish? The theme started with students increasing their self-understanding and their understanding of learning styles. The theme linked students' understanding to concepts of race and lifestyles in the broader global community. Students worked in cooperative groups to collect and graph data. They investigated accomplishments of famous individuals, learned the steps of report writing, evaluated others' reports, and shared their information with the class. Students studied the workings of their own bodies. They analyzed and evaluated data. They organized it and synthesized it into a new form for presentation to the class.

"The renewed trend in the schools toward interdisciplinarity will help students better integrate strategies from their studies into the larger world."

— *Heidi Hayes Jacobs*[16]

The human brain seeks to make meaning from new information or experiences; this meaning always relates to what is already known. An Interdisciplinary thematic curriculum facilitates learning by aiding the brain's connection making process of identifying patterns and relationships.

The People theme gives a clear focus while it interconnects a wide variety of important concepts for my students. It focuses first on the individual and expands outward to the world. It is broad enough to follow my students' interests and concise enough to deal with our district's curriculum objectives. Thematic teaching helps my students link what they already know to many different disciplines and subjects.[17]

∞

[1] Michael Caduto and Joseph Bruchac, *Keepers of the Earth: Native American Stories and Environmental Activities for Children* (Fulcrum: 1989). The stories are also available on audio tape.

[2] *How to Integrate the Curricula*, by Robin Fogarty (Skylight: 1991), p. 55.

[3] This is a central theme in the secondary school movement stimulated by Ted Sizer. For newsletter write the Coalition of Essential Schools, Box 1938, Brown University, Providence, RI 02912.

[4] Madeline Hunter, *Mastery Teaching* (TIP Publications: 1988).

[5] Bernice McCarthy and Susan Leflar, *4MAT In Action* (EXCEL, Inc.: 1988). This system will be discussed in Chapter 3, on learning styles.

6 For Further information see Gabriele Lusser Rico's *Writing the Natural Way* (Tarcher: 1983).

7 Nancy Margulies, *Mapping Inner Space* (Zephyr Press: 1991), presents a new visually graphic form of mind mapping called mindscapes.

8 Beck and Beck, p. 64.

9 Abraham Maslow, *Toward a Psychology of Being* (Litton Educational Publishing: 1968), Chapter Four.

10 Eva Knox Evans, *All About Us* (Golden Press, New York: 1968), Peter Spier, *People*, (Doubleday: 1990), and Ben Bova, *The Weather Changes Man* (Addison-Wesley, 1974).

11 Roberts and Guttormson, *You and Your Family: A Survival Guide for Adolescence* (Free Spirit Publishing: 1990), pp. 2-9, have graphic illustrations of 13 family styles rather than just a two-parent organization.

12 E. Aaronson, *The Jigsaw Classroom* (Sage Publications: 1978).

13 Simon Boughton's *Great Lives* (1989) is a good resource for brief vignettes.

14 Free Spirt Publishing has a number of helpful books for students: *Kids with Courage, True Stories About Young People Making A Difference*, and *The Kid's Guide to Social Action* by Barbara Lewis, and *Kid Stories, Biographies of 20 Kids You'd Like to Know*, by Jim Delisle. Write for a catolog to: Free Spirit Publishing, 400 First Street, Suite 616, Minneapolis, MN 55401-1724.

15 Sherry Fraser, project director, *Spaces* (Dale Seymour Publications: 1982).

16 Heidi Hayes Jacobs has an excellent book on the design and implementation of thematic units: *Interdisciplinary Curriculum: Design and Implementation* (ASCD: 1989). It is available from the Association for Supervision and Curriculum Development, 1250 N. Pitt Street, Alexandria, VA 22314.

17 For further development, read *Integrated Thematic Instruction: The Model*, by Susan Kovolic (Books for Educators, P.O. Box 20525, Village of Oak Creek, AZ 86341).

Learn Their Styles:
Improve Their Success

Defining learning styles ... Sensory perceptions ... Dunns' Model ... Teaching about styles ...
Hemispheric processing, the right and left ... Carbo's RSI ...
Butler's SDI ... McCarthy's 4MAT ... Others.

Thirty children and myself. Thirty different individuals and I intend to reach them all. I will help each grow in their skills, and in the sheer enjoyment of learning. In order to do this I must know my students. The better I understand my students the better I can plan the optimal learning environment for each child. Learning style systems give me the language to see differences in the basic ways children approach life and learning. This chapter explains learning style systems and their application with children in my classroom.

The National Association of Secondary School Principals defined Learning Styles in 1983.

> Learning style is that consistent pattern of behavior and performance by
> which an individual approaches educational experiences. It is the composite
> of characteristic cognitive, affective, and physiological behaviors that serve
> as relatively stable indicators of how a learner perceives, interacts with, and
> responds to the learning environment. It is formed in the deep structure of
> neural organization and personality which molds and is molded by human
> development and the cultural experiences of home, school, and society.[1]

An individual's learning style is determined by the interplay of his brain (the hardware) and his experiences (the software). Students cannot willfully change their learning styles to fit a school or a teacher.

I've heard teachers comment, "There are so many learning style systems I don't know which one is right. I don't know where to start." My own district convened a learning styles committee only to disband a few months later, giving up in despair while asking the same question. "Which one is right?"

The question is not "Which is right?" The question is which system do you want to start learning. All systems are based on respect for all learners. All systems focus on the learner's strengths rather than weaknesses. All systems help me be more observant of my students' styles, and more deliberate in planning to meet the needs of all students. Different systems allow me to look at different aspects of my students' learning styles. Each system has its place in helping me go beyond my own natural style, developing increased "style-flex" to better educate all students.

∞

Sensory perceptions are the brain's window to the outer world. We learn by hearing, seeing, touching, and smelling. The auditory sense is often the major one used in school, with visual stimulation second and lastly the sense of touch (tactile) or movement (kinesthetic). Many adults do not understand which of their senses they rely on the most. It is an important insight for learning.

Learning by hearing, auditory processing, is my weakest sense. I "hear" just fine, but I don't remember or process information well just by hearing. When the grocery clerk states my total bill, I hear the amount but I need to look at the register before I know what to write on my check. This is an obvious clue to me now, but I was thirty-some before I understood this meant I process information visually. Prior to understanding perceptual modalities I wondered what was wrong with me. I felt "dumb". Now I have learned coping skills; I take notes during a lecture so I can "see" what's being said. I write down items on a shopping list, but don't need the list to shop. The process of writing it down is enough to trigger my memory.

Julie is an example of a strong visual learner in my class. She learns by seeing. She reads rapidly, focusing on the whole thought rather than individual words. She translates the words into visual images naturally.

Julie taught herself to read when she was quite young. She remembers the shape configuration of words, along with her picture image of the real-life thing. Phonics has little meaning to Julie; she learns new words by sight. Like many visual learners she has a larger reading vocabulary than speaking vocabulary. She understands the meaning of words in print but since the words are not vocalized she may not know how to pronounce them.

About 40% of school-age children are visual processors. They gain information by observing and seeing. Visual learners tend to remember faces rather than names. They often make lists, web story ideas, and doodle when bored. When a child asks me to spell a word, I must write it down or use my visual imagination.

My classroom reflects my visual style. The room is visually pleasant to me, with clearly organized materials. Cozy corners and work areas are defined by color. The chalkboard has clear space for me to sketch concepts, web ideas, and write important words as we have group discussions.

Auditory learners have the advantage during lectures. About 20% of school age children are auditory learners. In my classroom Sharon typifies an auditory learner. She is good in phonics because she clearly hears the variety of sounds comprising a word. She likes oral spelling bees and studies her spelling by repeating the letters aloud. She often sub-vocalizes when reading "silently". She talks to herself as she plans and organizes. Sharon learns effectively in small group discussions, but may become distracted by surroundings sounds. Once I insisted Sharon take notes during a film only to have her later tell me that the note-taking got in the way of her listening. (Taking notes is the way I, a visual learner, remember what I hear.) Researcher John Goodlad found that 70% of instructional time was spent on "talk".[2] Lectures are effective for auditory learners — but most students are not auditory learners.

The tactile/kinesthetic learner learns by actively touching and moving. All of us began as tactile/kinesthetic learners, vigorously exploring the physical world. The younger the child the more likely he learns best by touching and moving. This first way of perceiving information continues to be the dominant mode for about 15% of adults. Tactile/kinesthetic people tend to be athletes, dancers, performers, skilled construction workers, and mechanics.

"If educators invested a fraction of their energy on stimulating the students' enjoyment of learning that they now spend in trying to transmit information we could achieve much better results."
— *Mihaly Csikszentmihalyi*

To learn, the kinesthetic learner must do. In my classroom Mike typifies a tactile/kinesthetic learner. He always seems to have his fingers doing something. He is completely engrossed when exploring the science materials. He tends the pond water and sets up the microscopes. He beams when he works with lego logo. He creates complex designs with the attribute blocks. He constructs with wood, or clay, or wire. He enjoys setting up the film machine and using a video camera. He is intensely engaged whenever the task involves moving. Tactile/kinesthetic learners must work with manipulatives to internalize concepts.

Unfortunately many traditional school activities are not very kinesthetic. Mike has trouble sitting still to read. Even action-oriented books don't keep Mike's attention because he doesn't want to read about the action, he wants to be in the action! "Reading is boring," he complains as he fidgets. He is very distractible. Sometimes it helps T/K learners to move a finger or a card under the words while reading. It's not much movement but for some learners it's better than nothing.

Often kinesthetic learners are poor spellers. They do not use the visual strategy of configuration or an auditory strategy of phonics. They have difficulty following lectures and discussions, because words have little meaning unless linked to experience.

Some Tactile/Kinesthetic learners are labeled "hyperactive" by adults who want students to sit still to learn. The kinesthetic learner isn't trying to be bad by moving about; she is marching to the rhythm of her own learning needs. She is the epitome of the old adage "I hear and I forget, I see and I may remember, I do and I understand."

Many of us have strengths in more than one sensory system. While I am a visual learner, I am also quite kinesthetic. When I present to educators at a conference I use visual overheads. I need to see what I am talking about. I also need to move around as I speak. I hate being confined to a podium and microphone; it cramps my style and I can't think as clearly. The movement helps my thoughts flow.

People who take in information well through all of their senses have the easiest time learning in school. No matter how material is presented multi-modality people are able to internalize it. The students who have the most difficulty learning tend to be low in all sensory processing. No matter how the material is presented these children find it difficult.

Growing Up Learning[3] is a helpful book about perceptual modali-

> "In our research we find quite simply that there is a real equation between the ability to entertain and sustain complex thinking processes and the richness of the person's sensory and kinesthetic awareness."
>
> — *Jean Houston*

ties. It is very readable and has checklists for adults and children. A 30 minute sound filmstrip explaining many of the concepts is available.[4] It is appropriate for training teachers. The company also sells a manipulative kit which is statistically reliable to evaluate the strength of a student's auditory, visual and tactile/kinesthetic short term memory. This individual evaluation, validated for preschoolers through adults, takes about 20 minutes. In my classroom I use a self report questionnaire for all students. If the results don't match with my observations of the student, I administer the individual assessment.

Because I'm a visual learner and seeing is the dominant way I learn, I have a tendency to use phrases like "I see . . ." or "It is clear . . ." Seeing words such as "in focus" creep into my language pattern, even though I may really mean the process of hearing. Auditory people tend to use phrases like "Now, listen to this," or "I'd like to use you as a sounding board". Tactile/kinesthetic people are prone to use word like "grasp" or "in touch with". As you listen to students you may hear clues to their processing by recognizing the language patterns. When I'm tuned into the language patterns of a particular student I am able to phrase my words to better connect with their modality language pattern. NeuroLinguistic Programming (NLP) describes further connections of language and modality.[5]

Accelerated learning techniques also incorporate a multi-modality approach. SALT techniques of physical and mental relaxation[6] include music, dramatic presentations, memory associations, and games to facilitate efficient learning which is also fun.

How do I accommodate all sensory styles in my classroom? I accommodate styles by thoughtful reflection on my students' needs and careful planning. I present information and provide practice using all sensory modalities. My job is to educate all of my students, not just the ones who fit my natural sensory style. Students cannot change their dominant sensory modality. It is my responsibility to teach the way each student can learn.

∞

Dunns' Learning Styles Model[7] identifies twenty-two factors in a person's learning style. The factors fall into five groups: environmental,

"In the future, we shall measure our lives by our own growth and our ability to help others grow."
— *Robert Theobald*

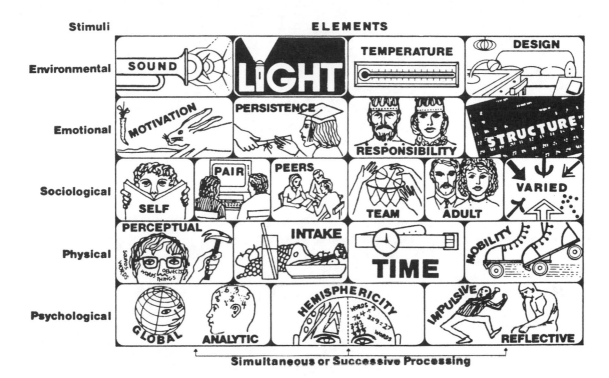

Stimuli	ELEMENTS			
Environmental	SOUND	LIGHT	TEMPERATURE	DESIGN
Emotional	MOTIVATION	PERSISTENCE	RESPONSIBILITY	STRUCTURE
Sociological	SELF	PAIR	PEERS / TEAM	ADULT / VARIED
Physical	PERCEPTUAL	INTAKE	TIME	MOBILITY
Psychological	GLOBAL / ANALYTIC	HEMISPHERICITY		IMPULSIVE / REFLECTIVE

Simultaneous or Successive Processing

emotional, sociological, physical and physiological. Their self-report inventory is validated for 3rd through 12th graders and can be computer scored. Dunns' system has been used for almost twenty-five years. Research studies done at over eighty-five colleges and universities have resulted in a wealth of data confirming the importance of adjusting for Dunns' learning style factors to improve success rates.

When I talk to teachers about this system I ask, "How many of you are morning people, you have the most energy in the morning, and think the best?" Many raise their hands. "How many of you are night people?" Other hands go up. The demonstration is simple. Research investigations confirm that peak/low energy patterns do have an effect on learning. Yet many educators act as if they believe children aren't effected by peak and low energy times.

My son, now twenty-three, has always been a night person. When he was young I could get him to go to bed but he didn't sleep. He was wide awake when I, a morning person, was absolutely exhausted. Unfortunately his high school classes began at 7:20 A.M. He needed to catch the school bus at 6:45 AM. I was bright-eyed; he was not. I cringed when he was assigned his hardest subject during that first hour in the

LEARNING STYLES MODEL
Designed by
Dr. Rita Dunn
Dr. Kenneth Dunn

"Learners can be helped to assess their preferred learning styles and strengths, and then taught ways to adapt the learning situation so that they use their strengths and work to improve their weaker areas."
— *Colin Rose*

morning. There was no way he would be alert. He could not change his biological clock. The Reptilian brain is responsible for our biological clocks; it's not a willful individual decision.

Food intake is another factor. Some individual's metabolism seems to function well on three meals a day. Others do not. Most teachers approve of feeding children breakfast at school if children are hungry. But after breakfast most schools expect students not to eat until the scheduled lunch.

My daughter taught me the silliness of this expectation. No matter how hard I tried to convince her to "eat your whole meal," it didn't work. Her grandfather was adamant that she sit at the table until she ate her entire meal. But she was not comfortable eating as much as I, or her grandfather, thought she should. Of course in two hours she was famished. Now, dietitians tell us that "grazing through the day" is probably wiser, provided the food is healthy. What about the child whose stomach isn't comfortable with a large quantity of food? Do we expect them to continue learning effectively without nourishment? In my classroom students snack on healthy foods. Of course, students need to clean up their food mess in the classroom, but this is no different than my expectation that they clean up their paper and pencil mess.

Four factors are in Dunns' Environmental category: sound, light, temperature and design. Silence drives some people crazy; they do better with some background sounds. But background noise drives other people crazy. Headphones can help in both cases. They can be switched off and worn to block out noise or they can be hooked up to focusing music.

Dunns' research demonstrates that learning is easier in the right environment. If you like bright light, you'll work best in bright light. Bright light, however, exhausts me. I work better in softer light and rarely have both rows of fluorescent lights turned on in my classroom.

Being too hot or too cold is often the easiest factor to deal with in school. Simply encourage students to dress differently. It sends shivers down my spine to see Matt wear T-shirts everyday in our Minnesota winter, but he is perfectly comfortable. I must remember not to project my own preferences on my students.

The design of furniture in the classroom is the last factor in this category. Some people think best and study best at a table; others prefer

to study on soft furniture. Over the years I have collected a small couch, a stuffed chair and six big floor pillows. My school engineers were originally appalled at anything other than traditional desks but, as time wore on, they accepted my nonstandard furniture. Our classroom atmosphere is softened by the furniture. It helps to make a more inviting and interesting classroom which meets my students' needs.

The research is similar for the Emotional factors — structure, motivation, persistence and responsibility. If you get what you need — a lot of structure or a little structure, you do better. While I was learning to help students make their own decisions, I made the mistake of responding to all students, "Do your best" or "What do you think needs to be done next?" As I began to internalize student styles I realized some students need very concrete answers to their "structure" inquiries, "Your story should be four pages."

Motivation, another factor, is significantly intertwined with students' past experiences and their prior knowledge. Adults are poorly motivated by situations in which they've already felt failure. And, adults are poorly motivated to learn new concepts when they have no idea how these concepts apply in their lives. Do students have a different base of motivation than adults? I think not. Past experiences and links to prior knowledge effect motivation.

Dunns' extensive work has made it clear that impersistent students do better when they are given breaks so they don't have to persist too long. They learn more. Breaks in my classroom may be getting a snack or "messing with" the water table where there are cups, pints, quarts, and gallons. When the classroom environment matches the individual student's style, the student does better.

As an adult it is my responsibility to teach, shop for groceries, balance my checkbook, wash the clothes, and keep our home clean. Sometimes I just don't have the time and energy to deal with all of my responsibilities. I have to make choices. What can I let go for a few days? If shopping for groceries is most important, I may delay washing clothes. Students make the same decisions. If playing with friends or talking on the phone seem more important to the student's life, that becomes the priority. Children make decisions on what's important just as I do. The issue is rarely whether the student is acting responsibly but rather it is a question whether the student's priorities are the same as the expectations. When a student is very responsible getting to softball practice but forgets his homework, I reflect on the possible reasons behind the behavior.

The Dunns' sociological component focuses on whether a person prefers to work alone, with one individual, or a group. Cooperative group work is wonderful for students who learn best talking to others. In addition, some students prefer to work directly with a teacher ("I love it when the teacher works specially with me!"), while others freeze up ("If the teacher would just go away I'd be able to think!")

I introduce the discussion of different learning styles in our classroom by polling students' food preferences. "How many of you like tomatoes? How many of you like peas? What about bananas? . . . Is it right or wrong to like one food but not another? . . . Of course not. It's also not right on wrong to prefer different ways of learning. What is important is that you figure out the best way for you to learn."

I hand out the leaflet I created about the different factors the Dunns identified. Students mark the form as we discuss differences. I graph some student preferences to illustrate the diversity, then guide them through an imagery allowing them to visualize their ideal learning environment. Afterwards the children draw and write about the perfect learning environment they have imagined. They include the factors of light, sound, time of day, people with them, and the types of materials available. My students proudly post their pictures and descriptive paragraphs in the hall for all to see. At open house the display provides stimulating conversations between parents and students.

In the next few weeks I use class time to develop a thoughtful reflection of homework habits and learning styles. When I teach second to fourth graders I use an illustrated story titled *Elephant Style*[8] which describes two best friends, Ellie and Fonty, and their differing learning styles. It is important for each child to know it is OK to be different. I want each student to be who she really is, rather than spend time and energy trying to figure out who she "should be". A filmstrip *Homework and Learning Styles*[9] is appropriate for fourth - seventh graders. For sixth - eighth graders I use the up-beat video, *Personal Learning Power*,[10] featuring multi-cultural high school students singing and dancing about their learning style power (Dunns' learning style factors).

St. John's University's Center for the Study of Learning and Teaching Styles has developed multiple resources available for parents and teachers who want to increase student achievement through awareness of the Dunns' learning style factors.[11]

"Making students more aware of their own study methods and learning styles allows them to control their activities more consciously."

— *Noel Entwistle*

-∞-

Hemispheric Processing is the last factor in Dunns' Learning Styles Model. Simultaneous, global thinking is a right hemisphere process while sequential, analytic processes are left hemisphere thinking. We are always whole-brained. The human brain works as a unit, never separated into isolated hemispheres or sections. However, individuals tend to favor one type of processing. One person may do better at sequential tasks and another person better with global tasks. Hemispheric processing strengths can be observed in students or a formal evaluation can be completed by a school psychologist using the *Kaufman Sequential or Simultaneous*.[12] The *K-SOS* gives a series of right and left hemisphere tasks. The result documents the student's relative processing strengths.

New technology, such as the PET scan, allows physicians to literally see the brain working. The procedure traces radioactively tagged blood as the brain "thinks" and records the brain's activity as a colorful video-tape.[13]

Many important language processes are facilitated by the left hemisphere. This hemisphere has a distinct area for understanding sound/symbol phonemes (Wernicke's area) and another controlling the creation of sounds (Broca's area). The left hemisphere is the expert on details and auditory distinctions. It prefers a literal interpretation, a clear straight forward reality. The left hemisphere favors objective and convergent thinking while the right hemisphere processes subjective and divergent thoughts.

The right hemisphere can recognize simple concrete words, and words with distinctive meanings like "dinosaur", but it does not distinguish between similar words like "than" and "then". The right hemisphere also controls voice intonation. It deciphers figurative language and metaphors; it understands innuendoes and humor. The left hemisphere, with its sequential processing, deals with past, present and future. It is time oriented. The right hemisphere lives in the timeless eternal present.

The right hemisphere deals with global ideas, seeing the whole forest rather than individual trees. It processes visual and spatial stimuli. Yet visual arts are not totally a right hemisphere task. If I teach art as a series of prescribed steps, it is a sequential left hemisphere process. If I go into an art museum and analyze the paintings according to a set of criteria, my left hemisphere dominates. If I go into the same museum and "oo and ahh" over a painting that profoundly affects me, my nonverbal, holistic right hemisphere is dominating.

The nonverbal right hemisphere works with imagery and affirmations. Athletes have used imaging for years. Olympic champions are groomed with imagery. PET scans have identified the physical effect of the use of imagery. When a physical movement is imagined, motor-neurons are actually firing, and thus programming in the brain. The physical activity is only imagined but the brain is being stimulated in the same manner as actually doing the physical movement.[14]

I use affirmations (positive self talk)[15] with students right from the first of the year. Students draw pictures and write about achieving their goals. Older students who have never used affirmations may be skeptical, but students who have used affirmations know they are helpful. Affirmations subtly but effectively prepare the mind for success.[15]

Our technological society has favored the detailed objective, sequential thinker over the right hemisphere's holistic intuitive processing. Some writers believe this over-emphasis, or dominance of left-hemi-

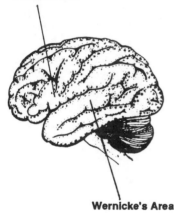

Broca's Area

Wernicke's Area

"The most important educational goal is learning to learn."
— *Luis Alberto Machado*

sphere strategies, has contributed to the decline of our economic system. Whole-brain strategies are more effective that just left-brain strategies.

Schools have also emphasized left-hemisphere processes over right hemisphere processes. Language instruction traditionally focused on detailed rules and grammar. Math was taught as sequential rules without internal understanding. Even geometry, the study of space, used sequential theorems rather than visual/spatial manipulatives. One local high school offers two types of geometry, the traditional theorem method and another which uses manipulatives for the "less able math student". In our schools there has been only one correct way to learn, the left hemisphere's way.

In 1985 the Educational Testing Service documented that students' visual abilities have declined over the past twenty years. This is probably because schools have ignored visual thinking. Art of all types, whether music, drama or visual art has been the first to be cut as school budgets declined. Yet for our engineers, architects, and surgeons visual thinking skills are crucial.

Dr. Roger Sperry, the Nobel prize recipient for his split brain research which contributed to right/left hemisphere insights, said in 1977 at the Smithsonian Institution,

> One important outcome (of the split brain research) is the increased insight and appreciation, in education and elsewhere, for the importance of nonverbal forms and components of learning, intellect, and communication. By the early 1970's it already had become evident, from the standpoint of brain research, that our educational system and modern urban society generally, with its heavy emphasis on linguistic communication and early training in the three R's, tends increasingly to discriminate against the nonverbal half of the brain, which has its own perceptual-mechanical-spatial mode of apprehension and reasoning. The amount of formal training given to the right hemisphere functions in our public school traditionally has been almost negligible, compared to that devoted to the specialities of the left hemisphere.[16]

Sperry recognized the over-emphasis of left hemispheric functions more than twenty years ago. It is time to change. It is time to understand the whole brain and re-balance the educational scale for children.

LEFT BRAIN	RIGHT BRAIN
Speaking	Intonation
Writing	Visual / Spatial
Objective	Subjective
Convergent	Diivergent
Sequential	Holistic
Analytical	Creative
Logical	Intuitive
Practical	Humor
Detail	Metaphor

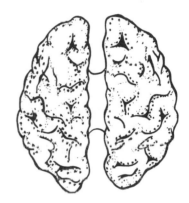

The full education of African Americans, Native Americans and Hispanics is a national concern. Studies indicate that minority cultures in the United States tend to favor right hemisphere, field-dependent processes while our educational system favors left-hemisphere processes.[17] One study comparing over 1000 adults concluded that Hopi Indians and urban blacks rely on right hemisphere strategies significantly more than urban whites.[18] An extensive review of research concluded that Native Americans favor right hemisphere strategies.[19] These studies do not label individuals; there are always individual differences. However the implications lead me to wonder whether our educational system has unknowingly discriminated by emphasizing left-hemisphere strategies with students whose style is the opposite. Have we unintentionally favored one cultural thinking pattern at the expense of other important kinds of thinking?

There are an increasing number of non-technical resources to help parents and teachers encourage both types of thinking. Some learning style systems speak directly of global/analytic styles while others deal with the issue without labels. *Is the Left Brain Always Right?*[20] is a quality resource for understanding pre-school and primary children. *Your Child's Growing Mind*[21] has an excellent chapter titled "Bridging the Hemispheres". *Teaching for the Two-Sided Mind*[22] was one of the first practical books and remains a classic in right brain activities. *Playing Smart*,[23] designed as a "parents guide to enriching offbeat learning activities for ages 4 - 14", provides whole brain activities without identifying hemispheres.

Carbo's Reading Style Indicator[24] applies the Dunn factors in the context of teaching reading. It especially focuses on the global vs. analytic dimension of reading and also on the preference for different sensory modes; particularly the auditory, visual, and tactile/kinesthetic. Marie Carbo believes that phonics, an auditory sequential method, is overused in our schools to the detriment of global learners. She categorizes reading approaches according to their hemispheric and sensory perceptual strengths.

The reading style materials sensitize educators to the differences between global and analytic reading strategies. The book, *Teaching Students to Read Through Their Individual Learning Styles*,[25] by Marie Carbo, Rita Dunn and Kenneth Dunn has practical teacher-tested methods of teaching reading to global learners and tactile/kinesthetic learners. In her recorded book method students listen to a tape of their teacher reading the short section. The students read and reread a short selection to themselves until they are able to read it smoothly.

My students taking Carbo's Reading Style Indicator (RSI) are excited to share the computer printout with their parents. The printout provides extensive information about all the Dunn elements of learning styles and provides a list of appropriate reading methods for the individual student. The computer printout was particularly helpful as I began learning more about teaching students with reading problems.

-∞-

Kathleen Butler's Style Differentiated Instruction has its roots in Gregorc's work, The Energic Model of Style.[26] It is a four quadrant system based on differing perception abilities from concrete to abstract and ordering abilities from sequential to random. These indicate four unique styles or viewpoints. According to this system the concrete sequential learner is "practical, predictable, to-the-point, organized and structured." The abstract sequential learner is "intellectual, logical, conceptual, rational and studious." Abstract random individuals are "emotional, interpretative, sensitive, holistic and thematic." The final group, the concrete random thinkers are "original, experimental, investigative, option-oriented and risk taking."[27]

Butler's system is designed for people ages thirteen through adult. Her book stresses the need for teachers to understand their own style and how it is reflected in their curriculum and teaching. Chapters describe both teachers' and learners' styles with clarity. Butler's suggestions deal with the needs of different perceptual modalities and the hemispheres. She has also produced an 85 page guide on learning styles which is appropriate to use with junior or senior high school students.[28] The guidebook provides an excellent opportunity for teachers and students to understand learning styles together, with the same system and the same language.

-∞-

The 4MAT System, developed by Bernice McCarthy in 1972, is "an eight-step cycle of instruction that capitalizes on individual learning

"Students took a long time to arrive at where they are today, and they will also require time to change."
— *Purkey and Novak*

"Teaching style is a set of attitudes and actions that open a formal and informal world of learning to students. It is a subtle force that influences students access to learning and teaching by establishing perimeters around acceptable learning procedures, processes, and products."
— *Kathleen Butler*

styles and brain dominance processing preferences."[29] 4MAT has roots as a system of learning styles, but has since been shown to be a very powerful model for curriculum planning.

McCarthy's system is based on perceiving and processing continuums which are juxtaposed to create four quadrants. Each quadrant is split into left and right brain sections creating the eight step cycle. This 4MAT cycle reflects the very natural process by which we learn.[30] Hence, lessons conceived and planned within the 4MAT framework are more readily absorbed and retained by students.

Quadrant One connects the lesson to students' prior knowledge and personal backgrounds. It is a time of sharing and reflecting. This step is critical to "hook" the brain and tune it in. In order to organize the new material effectively the brain must understand what the new information will connect with. Often this step has been ignored in traditional lessons.

Quadrant Two integrates the reflections and connects to new concepts or skills. The teacher is providing direct instruction in this quadrant. In Quadrant Three students practice new skills and begin to understand how the concepts fit into their lives. Quadrants Two and Three have traditionally been in our classrooms. The teachers "teach" and the students "practice".

Quadrant Four emphasizes higher level thinking skills. Here the students are asked to compare, analyze, evaluate and create. In this quadrant students apply their learning to new situations. Quadrant Four helps students make the learning their own.

In each quadrant students should experience both right and left hemisphere activities. The sequence of right and left activities through the four quadrants allows individual students to shine where the system matches their style yet stimulates students' areas of weakness. Presentation of course content through the 4MAT cycle provides a balanced set of experiences for the learner.

I have used 4MAT as the working framework of my interdisciplinary thematic curriculum for years. It provides a good basis for integration of themes as well as for assessment of performance. Most importantly, the 4MAT cycle of instruction enables my students to connect with their studies in personally relevant and meaningful ways.

This system, designed to address all learning styles, has similarities to the work of Madeline Hunter. Hunter devotes a chapter in *Mastery*

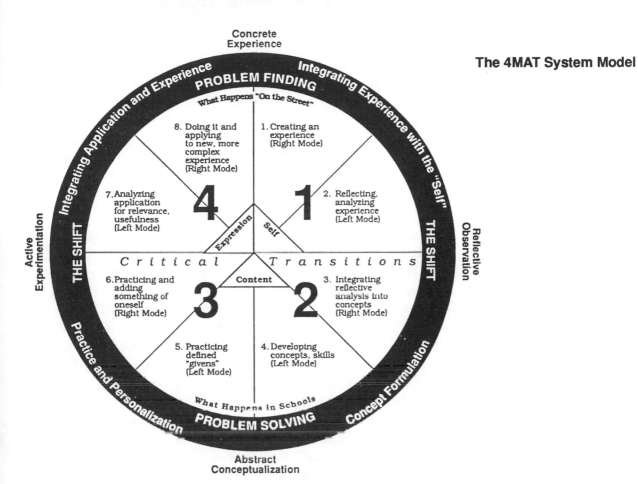

Concrete Experience

PROBLEM FINDING

What Happens "On the Street"

Integrating Application and Experience

Integrating Experience with the "Self"

8. Doing it and applying to new, more complex experience (Right Mode)

1. Creating an experience (Right Mode)

7. Analyzing application for relevance, usefulness (Left Mode)

2. Reflecting, analyzing experience (Left Mode)

4

1

Expression

Self

THE SHIFT

THE SHIFT

Active Experimentation

Reflective Observation

Critical   Transitions

Content

6. Practicing and adding something of oneself (Right Mode)

3. Integrating reflective analysis into concepts (Right Mode)

3

2

5. Practicing defined "givens" (Left Mode)

4. Developing concepts, skills (Left Mode)

Practice and Personalization

Concept Formulation

What Happens in Schools

PROBLEM SOLVING

Abstract Conceptualization

Teaching to "Teaching Both Halves of the Brain."[31] Hunter's anticipatory set, setting up the purpose of the lesson and connecting it with what the students already know, fits the realm of Quadrant One. Hunter's "giving information and modeling" are Quadrant Two activities. Student practice fits in the third quadrant while the last quadrant applies the concepts or uses the concept in a new way. For teachers evaluated with the Hunter system, 4MAT may be a useful adaptation to purposely include all learning styles.

I use the 4MAT cycle when I teach learning style concepts to other educators. First, teachers use one of the self report instruments to assess their own preferences. They are gaining an awareness of the instrument. This creates the personal meaning of Quadrant One and sets up WHY we need to understand different ways of learning. Next I address the question, "WHAT is this system about?" I give information, presenting the system's core concepts and assumptions. For a third quadrant activity I ask teachers to practice on their friends and loved ones to figure out HOW the system works. "What is your husband's learning style compared to your style? What is your daughter's? Your nephew's? Your friend's?" Teachers internalize aspects of the system and they learn more about the people they value. They come back with an increased belief in the importance of learning styles. Finally, the teachers take the concept into their classrooms. They apply the learning style concept to their real teaching situation. They evaluate, reflect and analyze their student styles. This begins to answer the question, WHAT IF I decide to plan for learning styles?

I use 4MAT to develop my interdisciplinary themes. In the People Theme I start with "Who are you?" We discuss, brainstorm, develop a ME story then share, comparing with others. The uniquely individual timelines begin with the present experience with students. When cooperative groups presented their research on human body systems the students used the first three quadrants. They pre-tested, discussed, taught using visuals and activities as well as giving information, and then checked for understanding. Later I had students take the information to the Fourth Quadrant by creating a "Learning Log" booklet of writing and drawings from the notes they took during the oral reports.

One of the beauties of the 4MAT system is its applicability to planning curriculum for every age of students in every subject area. There are many resources available enabling teachers to see examples of 4MAT lessons in their own area/grade level. One book incorporates visual thinking and art with the 4MAT system.[32] Another book on science gives examples at all grade levels. Two books present a wide variety of sample lessons in all subjects — primary phonics, concert band, geometric shapes, note-taking, and even teaching post-secondary attorney/client confidentiality.[33] 4MAT does a good job providing the structure to accommodate different learning styles.

-∞-

Three other "secondary through adult" systems are available — *NASSP's Learning Style Profile*,[34] Schmeck's *Inventory of Learning Processes* and Ned Herrmann's *Brain Dominance Instrument*.[35] NASSP's profile touches many learning style concepts. It covers a lot but is very time consuming to correct and glean meaningful learning style information. Schmeck's inventory uses self-report questions then sorts responses to determine if the student is a *deep-elaborative* or a *shallow-reiterative processor*. Schmeck believes shallow-reiterative students can be taught more effective, deep-elaborative thinking strategies. Herrmann's instrument is widely used in business and has the potential of being very useful in secondary schools.

There are many aspects of "learning styles." Each system has its usefulness. Each has its place to help educators understand students. I encourage you to begin learning any system which makes sense to you.

James Keefe, the Director of Research for the National Association of Secondary School Principals, sums up the importance when he writes "The key to effective schools is to understand the range of student learning styles and to design instruction and materials that respond directly to individual learning styles."[36] Thoroughly understanding any system will increase your ability to plan for greater success for students.

∞

[1] *Learning Styles Network Newsletter*, Summer 1983, Vol. 4. #2. Subscription to this newsletter is $10, published 3 times a year, St. John's University, Grand Central Pkwy., Jamaica, NY 11439.

[2] John Goodlad, *A Place Called School* (Institute for the Development of Educational Activities, Inc.: 1984), p. 229.

[3] Walter Barbe, *Growing Up Learning* (Acropolis Books: 1985).

[4] The filmstrip titled *A Common Sense Approach to Learning* can be purchased for $20.00 or loaned for 30 days. The Modality Kit is about $120.00. Zaner-Bloser, Inc., 2300 West 5th Ave., P.O. Box 16764, Columbus, OH 434216.

[5] John Grinder and Richard Bandler, *The Structure of Magic II* (Science and Behavior Books: 1976).

[6] SALT, the Society for Accelerative Learning and Teaching, 3028 Emerson Ave. S. Minneapolis, MN 55408 and Colin Rose, c/o ALS, 50 Aylesbury Rd., Aston Clinton, Aylesbury Bucky, England, HP225AH.

[7] Ken and Rita Dunn have written thirteen books on learning style issues, including, *Teaching Elementary Students Through Their Individual Learning Styles (3-6)* (Allyn & Bacon, Inc.: 1992), *Teaching Secondary Students Through Their Individual Learning Styles (7-12)* (Allyn &

Bacon, Inc.: 1992), and *Teaching Young Children Through Their Individual Learning Styles (K-2)* (Allyn & Bacon, Inc.: 1992). Their many books, videos, teaching materials and newsletter are available from St. John's University's Center for the Study of Learning and Teaching Styles, Utopia Pkwy., Jamaica, NY 11439.

[8] $12.00 from St. John's University's Center for the Study of Learning and Teaching Styles.

[9] Available from the St. John's University's Center for the Study of Learning and Teaching Styles, $40.00.

[10] *Personal Learning Power"* (15 Minutes, VHS) created by Kenneth Dunn is part of a package called *Amazing Grades*. For information write to Great Ocean Publishers, Inc., 1823 North Lincoln St., Arlington, VA 22207.

[11] St. John's University's Center for the Study of Learning and Teaching Styles, Utopia Pkwy., Jamaica, NY 11439.

[12] The K-SOS, a subtest on the K-ABC is available from American Guidance Service, Circle Pines, MN 612-786-4343.

[13] PET stands for positron emission tomography. Other types of technology are also capable of peering into the live brain. *Discover* magazine's special collector's issue No. 13, Winter 1990-91, called *Exploring the Mind* has a very readable article, "The Mind in Motion".

[14] *Discover* magazine, Winter 1990, p. 17.

[15] "Positive Self Talk" by Launa Ellison, *Teaching K-8*, August/September, 1987.

[16] Roger Sperry, "Consciousness, Personal Identity, and the Divided Brain," in *The Dual Brain*, (Guilford: 1985), p. 18.

[17] Warren TenHouten, "Cerebral-Lateralization Theory and the Sociology of Knowledge," *The Dual Brain* (Guilford: 1985), p. 353.

[18] Sally Springer and Georg Deutch, *Left Brain, Right Brain* (W.H.Freeman: 1985), p. 240.

[19] Arthur More, "Leaning Styles and Indian Students: A Review of Research" (1984), ERIC Document Ed 249 028.

[20] Cherry, Godwin and Staples, *Is the Left Brain Always Right?* (David Lake: 1989).

[21] Jane Healy, *Your Child's Growing Mind* (Doubleday: 1987).

[22] Linda Verlee Williams, *Teaching for the Two-Sided Mind* (Simon & Schuster: 1986).

[23] Susan Perry, *Playing Smart* (Free Spirit Publishing: 1990).

[24] All of the materials relating to Carbo's system are available from Learning Research Associates. P.O. Box 39, Roslyn Heights, NY 11577.

[25] Marie Carbo, Rita Dunn and Kenneth Dunn, *Teaching Students to Read Through Their Individualized Learning Styles* (Prentice Hall: 1986).

[26] Kathleen Butler, *Learning and Teaching Style In Theory and Practice* (The Learner's Dimension: 1986). 7 Lakeview Drive, Columbia, CT 06237.

[27] These four quotes are from Butler's book, pp. 18-19.

[28] Kathleen Butler, *It's All in Your Mind*. (The Learner's Dimension: 1988).

[29] Bernice McCarthy, "Using the 4MAT System to Bring Learning Styles to Schools," *Educational Leadership*, October 1990, p.31.

[30] Bernice McCarthy, *The 4Mat System: Teaching to Learning Styles with Right/Left Mode Techniques* (Barrington, IL: Excel, Inc., 1981, 1987). The chart on page 53 above is from this source.

[31] Madeline Hunter, *Mastery Teaching* (TIP Publications: 1982), p.39.

[32] Kathy Mason, *Beyond Words: The Art and Practice of Visual Thinking* (1989), available from Zephyr Press (602-322-5090).

[33] Available from Excel, Inc., 200 West Station St., Barrington, IL 60010. Their latest product *4MATION* is MacIntosh software designed to give educators step by step guidance.

[34] Available from National Association of Secondary School Principals, P.O. Box 3250, Reston, VA 22090.

[35] Available from The Brain Dominance Institute, 2075 Buffalo Creek Road, Lake Lure, NC 28746.

[36] *Student Learning Styles and Brain Behavior*, (1982), National Association of Secondary School Principals, 1904 Association Drive, Reston, VA 22091.

Personality in the Classroom: Their Needs and Mine

Extraversion and Introversion ... Sensing and iNtuitive ... Thinking and Feeling ...
Judging and Perceiving ... Combining factors NF, NT, SJ, SP ...
The student instrument ... Providing for different needs.

Parents know each child is uniquely different. Teachers have begun to understand the significant impact of students' cultural heritages, and teachers are increasingly aware of differing skill levels. But there is another difference embedded in everything we do. It is the student's personality type. Understanding personality type has given me the magic glasses to see through the fog of students' behaviors and plan for greater student success.

The Myers-Briggs Type Indicator (MBTI) was developed over a twenty year period beginning in the forties. It is based on concepts of Carl Jung. Over 12 million people, in the United States and countries around the world, have taken the indicator. The MBTI is the parent of a new personality instrument validated for students in second to eighth grades, the Murphy Meisgeier Type Indicator for Children[1] (MMTIC). This chapter explains personality type and its implications in my classroom.

-∞-

Extraversion and Introversion is the first continuum in the MBTI system. Extraversion/ Introversion indicates where "attention is focused" — on the external or internal world.[2] This difference has been noted by nurses caring for newborns. Some infants are calm and quiet, others immediately vocalize their needs. The difference seems to be linked to the brain's level of a particular neurotransmitter called dopamine.[3]

My 14 year old daughter is an Extravert. Her thoughts seem to flow out before she knows what she's thought. Extraverts verbalize in order to clarify their thoughts. They are stimulated by other people and activity. They tend to love shopping malls, sports arenas and theaters because they are energized by the activity. After a long hard day at school or work, extraverts prefer to renew their energy by going to a party.

Introverts are the opposite. Introverts need quiet alone time to renew. Crowds exhaust them. Introverts are energized by their internal world of ideas. They consider their thoughts carefully before verbalizing them. I am an Introvert. When something is important to me, I need to take my thought inside, reflect on it, understand the implications, and formulate my answer before I say anything. Thinking is a quiet reflective process for me before I speak.

It is important for me to remember that when my daughter speaks she is processing her thoughts. What she begins with is not her final conclusion, as mine is. She thinks as she speaks. We are different. The Myers-Briggs system gives me a way to understand our differences in a positive way. Neither of us are right or wrong, we are simply different.

I have worked with Extraverted principals who think out loud. They unknowingly send confused messages to the staff. Some colleagues understand the principal is just thinking aloud; others believe a decision has been made.

In my classroom Extraverts' hands shoot up first. They haven't thought of an answer but they know they have something to say. The Introverts are quieter. "Wait time" is crucial if I'm going to engage their brains. The Introverted child needs time to internally reflect on the question before he will risk raising his hand. I want to have Introverts involved so I encouragingly say, "Think about it a minute, I know you have thoughts to share too."

About 65% of people in the U.S. are Extraverts. Cooperative group strategies are a blessing to Extraverted students. They can legally talk in groups. They can openly share their ideas by thinking aloud as they work. This fits their natural style and they learn more.

My strong Extraverts have a lot of difficulty reading silently. During our daily super quiet uninterrupted reading time (SQUIRT) they ask to read to each other in the hall. They really do concentrate better when they read aloud. Accommodating extraverts creates an unquiet

"If man does not keep pace with his companions, perhaps it is because he hears a different drummer: Let him step to the music he hears, however measured or far away."
— *Henry David Thoreau*

"Allowing Extraverted children to study with friends often will increase their success in school — and will have other benefits as well. To begin with, it should increase enjoyment of learning."
— *Charles and Connie Meisgeier*

"I didn't belong as a kid, and that always bothered me. If only I'd known that one day my differences would be an asset, then my early life would have been much easier."
— *Bette Midler*

classroom, but it's a classroom where these students learn.

All assignments should not, however, be designed for students to work cooperatively. My Introverts need time away from the frenetic verbal pace of the extraverts' world. I respect their need to retreat into a private corner for their quiet, reflective think time. I show approval of their need for quiet by providing them with time and space. Introverts' real selves usually remain hidden, shared only with intimate, long trusted friends. It is likely I won't ever know my Introverted students as well as I know my Extraverts.

Both the Extravert and Introvert can make excellent presentations to large groups. It's the Extraverts natural style to talk with people but Introverts are quite capable of making presentations. Sometimes Introverts' presentations are smoother because, to be comfortable, they must be well prepared and have a clear concept of exactly what they are going to say.

Extravert/Introvert characteristics are taken into account within Dunns' Learning Style Model on sociological factors. Some students report they learn more working with others in a group; others prefer working alone or with one partner. This factor, the result of personality, originates deep within an individual's neural structure. I want all of my students to learn in the most effective way, thus, I plan for both types. Going against students' natural energy produces less learning.

∞

Sensing and iNtuition are the second pair of factors on the MBTI continuum. (The symbol for intuition is "N" because "I" already designates an Introvert.) This refers to the perceiving function which describes how an individual prefers to gather information.

Sensors make up about 70% of the U.S. population. These people learn by using their senses. They learn by "hands-on" experiences. For the Sensor doing is believing. These are practical students who learn new skills step by step, and enjoy using the skills they already know. They live in the here and now. Sensors attend to details, believe in facts and are comfortable with the traditional, familiar ways of doing things.

In the classroom my Sensors want specific directions, "Write a 3 page story." They want to experience and manipulate. "Cut up this circle into four equal pieces. What fraction name is one of the pieces?" Sensors need to concretely compare the wedges of 1/4 and 1/3 to internalize the difference between the fractions.

Strong sensors tend to prefer reading for practical, real-life information and may dislike novels. Sensors who are beginning readers tend to remember words related to concrete meaning such as "car", or "mom". Abstract words like "the" or "than" are harder for sensors to remember. They live in a literal world of concrete experience and include little fantasy in their play.

Reflect back to the discussion of perceptual modalities — the auditory, visual and tactile/kinesthetic senses. Since the Sensor gains information and learns primarily through his senses, it is critical that his strongest sensory modality be stimulated. If the student is a visual learner, his educational setting must be rich with colorful films, visual displays and demonstrations. If the student is a tactile/kinesthetic learner he must manipulate objects to learn. He must touch things, rearrange them, and work with them in order to understand the meaning in his body. When this sensory stimulation is absent the student can not learn effectively.

In my classroom, Sensors are very attracted to "stuff." They dive into every science investigation with "stuff" — microscopes, mystery powders, colored solutions. Math "stuff" such as GeoBlocks attracts them. They tend to be more uncomfortable with creative writing probably because of the lack of stuff. They ask for specific directions, "How long should my story be?" As an iNtuitive my natural response would be, "As long as it takes to develop the story." But since learning about type differences, I respond to Sensors, "Your story should be four pages." The Sensor is requesting specific directions and, to foster her success, I must give it.

In some classrooms Sensor students become educationally starved. They cannot maintain their focus on academic work without the sensory stimulation they require to interpret the world. Sensors have a significantly higher drop out rate than their counterparts, the iNtuitives. One study of 500 people who did not finish 8th grade found that 99% of the people were the Sensor type.[4]

INtuitive students (30% of the general population) tend to have the advantage in most educational settings. In a study of 3500 male high

"Provide (Sensors) with four or five practical examples each time a new concept is introduced. Relate the current task to real people, things, or places in the student's world."

— Meisgeier and Murphy

school students, iNtuitives consistently had higher grade point averages.[5] On an eighth grade Stanford Achievement Test the INtuitives scored significantly higher on all three math sections — computation, concepts and applications.[6] In another study iNtuitives mean score was 47 points higher than Sensors on the Verbal Ability SAT.[7] INtuitives understand where a lesson or test is going. They make links and connections to other information. These people are global learners who see the big picture. They like to imagine possibilities and improvise new strategies. They see patterns and relationships. They focus on concepts rather than details, often skimming over, or completely ignoring, directions. INtuitives seek new and better ways of doing something and they enjoy working with their hunches. They are future oriented rather than focusing on the here and now.

INtuitive students enjoy the expanse of our interdisciplinary themes because this allows them to link concepts. They often work in bursts of energy, followed by a less intense time. The less intense period is an incubation time, important for internal processing. INtuitives love to hypothesize during science, are full of ideas for solving the world's problems in social studies, and have little problem coming up with story ideas for writing. INtuitives pay little attention to details. They tend to be good readers and grasp meaning "between the lines". They usually read in chunks because they are seeking meaning rather than seeing individual words. Assigned projects for iNtuitives need to have enough breadth to allow them to dream up their own ways of doing the tasks.

I'm an iNtuitive person. It's in keeping with my personality type to write this book. My iNuitive nature focuses on the future. I see ways to improve the success rate of all students. I see the vision of tomorrow's education fostering success for every child by understanding our differences and planning more appropriate strategies for each learner.

∞

Thinking and Feeling make up the third continuum and describe how we organize information to make decisions. Both of these factors are thinking because they are decision-making modes. They simply consider different data to make the decision.

The Thinker personalities rely on objective, rational principles to

"The intuitive lives in anticipation. Whatever is can be better, or different, and is seen as only a way station."

— *Keirsey and Bates*

make decisions. They are interested in justice and fairness without personal involvement. These people believe policies, laws and rules are not to be bent or broken. They tend to be goal-oriented rather than people oriented. The Thinker is often good at evaluating and criticizing with analytical precision.

In my classroom these students constantly ask "Why?" "Why does the pulley change the force?" "Why does the division of fractions work that way?" "Why does the surface tension of liquids make a difference?" "Why do I have to do this assignment?"

These students love to debate issues. The Extraverted Thinker charges right into the debate; the Introverted Thinker plans and strategizes before she begins, but loves the debate challenge just as much. They debate non-smokers' rights, world news, and how to resolve Native American tribal claims.

Thinkers excel in classrooms where information gathering is the essence of success. The Thinker wants to be right, do the best work and receive the top grades. Other students' feelings are irrelevant since the Thinker is at school to learn the objective information. Impersonal math algorithms are no problem; they fit this student's style. Thinkers are task oriented, interested in cause and effect relationships, and the proof. Science, for Thinkers, is built on a series of clear facts to understand the universe. These students tend to view history without the grays of differing viewpoints. They don't tend to understand the alternative views presented by the multi-cultural and gender-fair advocates. They seek what they believe to be true and logical. Thinkers make decisions with their heads.

The strong Thinker often criticizes others by pointing out how the other is "wrong". They tend to use sarcasm or "put-downs" without understanding the pain they are causing others. Their friends are usually other Thinker students who are equally oblivious of their own poorly developed social skills.

Morgan and Matt are my two strongest Thinker types. They spend hours on the computer using a wide variety of software and creating their own programs. They get into raucous arguments over the "right" strategy to solve a logical word puzzle. They are forever setting up a new science experiment — the melting time of snow compared to ice, the arc of a pendulum with different weights, or creating a quadruple pulley system

"The Thinking-Feeling male-female dilemma haunts the workplace. The Thinking woman swims upstream against a rather swift negative current in most aspects of her life, especially in the workplace. If she is objective and decisive, she is viewed as "hard" and "unfeminine" and may be subject to a variety of even harsher names. The Feeling male is similarly presented with some special problems at work; he may be called a wimp simply for his caring nature."

— *Kroeger and Thuesen*

before my other students understand the effect of one pulley. Because they thrive on knowledge about how things work, they can easily leap over the heads of my other students. I need to be aware of this tendency, applaud their specific knowledge, yet ask them not to share their understandings immediately with other students. My other students need time to "construct" meaning for themselves not just be told how something works, even if the person telling is another student.

The Feeling personality uses a different set of criteria to make decisions. These people are very concerned about interpersonal relationships. They value harmony. They tend to be good at reading emotions and will modify rules because they understand the extenuating circumstances. They tend to be caring, empathic and appreciative. They base their decisions on how they and others will feel about the result. Young children are most often Feelers since the Thinking strategies, based on rules and policies, are concepts learned later.

I need to remember to greet my Feeler students as they arrive at school in the morning. If I don't they will believe I "don't like them". I also need to remember to make personal, positive comments about their work, "Nice job!" "I really like the way you ...."

Feelers tend to like cooperative group work, but are easily upset when group members are not harmonious. They are sympathetic and honestly care about others' viewpoints. These students tune into their schoolwork better when the topic connects to people and the human interest side of life. History, made alive with plays or role-playing, taps these students' natural interests. Historical novels are more appropriate for Feelers than the factual textbooks Thinkers prefer to use. Connecting scientific discoveries to the people who achieved the discovery is a good strategy for engaging Feelers. Asking "How did you like doing the experiment?" is important along with "What did you learn from the experiment?" Feelers decide with their hearts.

Remember that personality factors are not either/or but on a continuum. While individuals may favor one strategy, they use both in their daily lives, but probably not to the same extent.

Adrienne and Rachel are strong Feelers. They simply cannot focus on their schoolwork unless their feelings are calm. Their concern for friends, feelings, fairness and justice is so great that they can easily become blocked and unable to concentrate on their academic work. In order to get them restarted, I have no choice but to deal with whatever the Feeling issue is. This means I stop my "teaching" focus and listen to their concerns. I facilitate problem-solving between them and friends, helping them give "I" statements. "I feel frustrated (or sad, or put-down or mad) when you ...."[8] If I ignore their feelings, they will remain unfocused on the academics and preoccupied with their people issue. They will not only "waste time" but will miss the content of my instruction. And, the Feeling issue will probably escalate and blow up during lunch or recess. It doesn't matter what lesson was supposed to be taught, I must deal with the feelings if I want either student to get unstuck and return their focus to their academic work.

In the U.S. population 60% of males and 40% of females are Thinkers; 40% males and 60% females are Feelers. This is the only continuum that has a male/female component. The strong Feeler male and the strong Thinker female often may feel like they are "swimming upstream" within the cultural patterns of our society.

The Thinking/Feeling difference can often be observed on the playground when boys stick by the rules of the game and girls change the rules to keep everyone happy. Carol Gillian, in her book *A Different Voice*, develops a rich understanding of this Thinking/Feeling decision-making difference in pre adolescent males and females.[9] Her work is important reading for middle school teachers.

∞

Judging or Perceiving (50-50%) are attitudes designated by the last scale. These attitudes indicate how we prefer to interact with our outer worlds, and are the most difficult qualities to hide.

Judgers prefer to make decisions using their Thinking or Feeling data. They like to be organized. They plan what needs to be done and accomplish it by the deadline. Judging students prefer an orderly routine, a clear structure and predictable environment. They usually have good study habits and regularly turn assignments in on time. Judging students find it easy to follow teachers' instructions. They may be externally motivated by a teacher's praise or a grade, or they may be internally motivated, living up to their own standards. Regardless they have a strong sense of the "right way" to do their school work.

Jessica is a strong Judger. She is uncomfortable when our schedule shifts and her work time is altered. She plans what she will accomplish each day and becomes frustrated if unforeseen factors block her plan. When she has a major project, she assigns herself dates for different parts of the project. She reviews her progress and monitors her work toward the goal as part of her natural flow. Jessica's play is also organized. She is quite happy with her routine of swimming and tennis lessons. She is not comfortable simply "hanging out" with friends.

Jani is a strong Perceiver. She loves "hanging out" with her friends. She is full of ideas and curiosity. She's thoroughly involved with the here and now, delving into whatever is happening today. She enjoys her days without worrying about what's next. She enjoys games, and the breaks in our classroom routine.

Jani has a lot of different interests and often has a lot of projects going at once. She has difficulty narrowing her ideas to make a commitment to a particular long-term project and often is still deciding when other students have begun their work. When gathering information for a research project Jani may become perplexed. She has difficulty deciding which bits of information are important enough to write on a note card. She often ends up with too much information which is peripheral and then she doesn't have enough relevant information to finish her report. Her resulting report may have disconnected thoughts. I am aware of Jani's natural thinking pattern and give her extra support while she makes note cards. "Jani, before you write anything on a note card, ask yourself if this is new information and if it relates directly to your topic." I help her practice making decisions on the relevancy of the information. I touch base with Jani often during the report preparation process.

Jani doesn't have an internal mental map of the time it will take her to complete a long project. To insure her success, I help her think through the project's deadline and other time commitments in her life. I teach her to identify the due date and then plan her activities backwards from that time.[10] In other words, "Jani, the report is due on Wednesday. Do you have soccer or any other responsibilities on Tuesday night that will keep you from finishing your report? OK, how far do you think you need to be on Monday to be successful?" I check in with Jani often in order to insure her success and I verbalize the thinking strategies I want her to internalize.

Deadlines are difficult for Perceivers because they are busy perceiving the present moment. I encourage Perceivers learn to write down assignments and gently remind them of tasks so they can be successful. "Show me on your fingers, on a scale of 1-5, how far are you on ..." This does not mean I nag or "get on their case," but rather I nurture a thoughtful awareness of time-management. Because I want each student to be successful, I remember to give extra time and effort to teach Perceivers time-management skills, rather than let them flounder with assignment deadlines.

In a recent science class my students' personalities were stereotypically obvious. My Extraverts were verbalizing what they are thinking while my Introverts were quietly reflective. My Sensing students dove into the hands-on materials while requesting step by step directions. They forgot to create a hypothesis before they experimented because they wanted "to do". My iNtuitives formulated their hypothesis before touching their materials. Some of my feelers didn't start working because they didn't feel another child was fair. They wanted me to "talk to him" before they started working. They felt slighted and their investigation was blocked. Meanwhile my Thinkers were busily recording data and analyzing the experiment. My Judgers monitoring their progress and the length of their experiment, while my Perceivers were so involved with perceiving they lost sense of time and never finished the experiment.

-∞-

Combining the descriptors gives more insight about students. One survey of 150, 5-8th graders in my school found that 91% were Feeling-Perceivers. No wonder teachers were exhausted each afternoon. These students are most interested in each other and don't finish their assignments on time. Feeling and Perceiving both seem to have developmental implications. Young children don't begin making decisions by analyzing information, they react on a feeling level. Most children need to learn a sense of time, and experience the planning necessary to judge time factors adequately.

The iNtuitive-Feeling student represents 12% of the population and 36% of the teachers.[11] These people need to be appreciated; they are very

"'What time is it now?' Millie asked.
'Oh, I don't know, Millie, you just got here.'
'Momo, what time is it?'
'We have hours to play.'
'Momo,' said Millie, sounding irritated, 'what time is it exactly?'
'I can't tell you exactly because I have all the clocks set fast so that I can be on time.' "

— *Diane Farris*

sensitive to criticism. iNtuitive-Feeling teachers often individualize their instruction and are interested in developing their students' true potential. NF teachers tend to humanize many aspects of the curriculum. They help students understand the lives of great people and use math word problems which involve people. NF students often excel in social studies and the humanities possibly because they're people subjects. Only about 20% of school administrators are iNtuitive Feelers.[12]

INtuitive-Thinking students represent another 12% of the population. These students tend to be high achievers because they have a passion to know everything and they naturally make intuitive connections between realms of information. They may seem to be intellectually precocious and are often over-represented in "gifted" programs. INtuitive-Thinkers enjoy an intellectual debate, but tend not be in touch with their emotions. Only 6% of teachers are this type and usually are teaching in high schools or in "gifted and talented" programs, because they are interested in the development of intelligence. About 21% of school administrators are this type.

According to Kiersey and Bates, Sensing-Judging students represent about 38% of the students, 56% of the teachers and 55% of school administrators. These teachers run an orderly, efficient classroom. They carry on the traditions of the school, faithfully upholding the school's rules and policies. Sensing-Judging students are often believed to be "model" students. They like a predictable classroom routine. They are dependable and responsible. They prefer precise directions. They pay attention to details, do what they are told without questioning, and learn well with a sequential presentation of material.

David is a Sensing-Judging student in my classroom. He thrives on being told exactly what to do and how to do it. He is obedient and prides himself on the accuracy of his work. He always finishes his work on time. He is uncomfortable with open-ended situations or assignments. When I assign an open writing project, "This week write a short story," David asks for further directions. "What exactly do you want me to write about?"

The last combination, the Sensing-Perceiving personality, is also 38% of our students but only represented by 3% of the teachers and administrators. Because of their small numbers I rarely encounter SP teachers. But once, I presented a seminar at a nearby Arts high school.

Half of the staff in our meeting were SPs. These teachers thrive on plays, crafts, music and dance. SPs are free spirits who want lots of action, are bored with routine paper-pencil tasks and have trouble finishing things. They enjoy working with "stuff" and messing around with science experiments. They must have concrete, "hands-on" experiences to learn effectively. These teachers tend to run active, unpredictable classrooms and care little about school policies, educational theories or long-term goals.

Morgan is an ISTP. He sticks to a few good friends. He prefers to read only nonfiction and approaches his life from a rational, analytical base striving to figure out exactly how the world works. He consistently wants to work with "stuff" whether its the computer or the pendulums. He often surprises me with his latest invention or demonstration. I know he is learning, but he does not finish tasks on time. I know he's bright. I know he's capable. I also know he is a Perceiver. His mind is full of information but he does not do what is necessary to turn assignments in. He needs to learn how to cope with completing tasks, despite it not being a natural quality. I negotiate assignments and offer alternatives. But, in the end, its Morgan who must do the learning.

Jenny is an ENFJ. She has a wide variety of friends and connections all over the school. She ran a good campaign for student council and was elected. She sees ways to improve our school and wants others to understand her insights. She is a good committee chairperson because she remembers to get her committee together. They plan, make decisions and report back to the student body on time.

In some ways I think the ESFP personality is the hardest student type for me to educate. Is that because this student is my opposite? Probably yes! The Extraverted student needs to talk to process her thoughts. I need quiet to process my thoughts. The Sensing student needs concrete experiences, and in her particular perceptual modality, to internalize an experience. She needs specific and clear directions. My first tendency is to give broad directions to outline what needs to be done within a conceptual framework.

When writing I naturally choose the phrase, "I think ..." In most sentences it would be equally appropriate to choose "I feel ..." But my tendency is to evaluate all of the data in a rational way. Feelers decide on their actions according to how others may "feel" — not by their

"Many of a child's behaviors are predictable if you know his style profile. And, forewarned, you can more easily plan an effective learning program to reduce liabilities and increase assets."
— *Simon and Byram*

"rational thinking". Finally the ESFP type is busy perceiving the situation and generating possibilities rather than focusing on the task to be accomplished. In summary, the ESFP student's natural tendency would be to talk a lot, need concrete experiences, make decisions in relation to friends and not finish work on time. I have these students in my classroom. I will always have all types of students in my class. Since I am committed to teaching every student, I cannot simply teach in my natural style. I have developed teacher "style flex". I change my natural way to accommodate my students' needs. I set up an environment that promotes success for each type. I strive to do what is necessary to educate each student.

Elizabeth Murphy, author of *The Developing Child* and developer of the MMTIC, has written an insightful skit to help people understand teacher and student type.[13] Four "good teachers" (F,T,S, and N) begin by describing themselves. A Feeler teacher begins by saying, "I really care about my students' welfare. I want to be sure they learn but I also want them to have a good home, lots of happy experiences and feel good about themselves." Each teacher personality type explains its goals and lesson plans in about a page of script. All four types of students respond after each teacher type. The Feeling student loves the Feeling teacher and is able to learn in her classroom. Students of different types speak clearly of their frustrations and give advice on how they "wish" she would teach. The characters seem very real. The differences between teacher goals and instructional methods for each type are beautifully illustrated by this skit. The skit is a good staff development resource.

How do I deal with all personality types in my classroom?

I begin by telling my students about the MMTIC personality type system. I have my students take the inventory. "Today you are going to take a questionnaire about how you like to behave. There are no right or wrong answers for these questions. They're just questions about who you are." Then I teach a few students how to score their MMTIC using a calculator and the scoring templates.[14] These students run our "Personality Table" and help others to score their results. Students check their calculations twice, then enter their results on a student profile and on the appropriate square on a class personality bar graph. Finally, I ask students to verify the results by checking off the descriptors they agree with beneath each type. This is an important step for students to understand and decide if they agree with the results of the questionnaire.

After a few days all students have completed scoring their MMTIC forms. I read *Type Tales*,[15] a narrative about two imaginary dogs illustrating type differences. Then I discuss each of the type designations. During the next few weeks I deliberately set up like-type cooperative work groups for social studies and science projects. After each project we discuss the differences in the way type groups approached the activity.

Students learning about MMTIC personality types.

When I plan lessons, I provide flexibility in how to complete the tasks and give both general and specific directions. As we begin to study American history, for example, I start from the present, with what students have experienced. Then I have students find out what their parents have experienced and teach history backwards. Beginning with present experience is a more fruitful progression for concrete learners (S). I have taught students how to set up timelines before this by using their own lives (F). Now I ask them to create a timeline from 1950 to the present and put on it ten important things which happened. "You may ask other people like your parents or grandparents (F) or you may use the resource books in the corner (T). Figure out how at least three events were connected to each other (N)." The directions are specific enough

"Although it is never easy to change one's own behavior, Style-Flex is no more difficult to learn than the other methods' you mastered as part of your preparation for teaching. It means learning to look through the 'window on the world' of the person you are talking with, and learning to see what he sees. As a teacher, it means helping your student to understand your goals in his framework, and helping him to reach them. It also means learning to understand his goals, and helping him reach those, too."

— *Simon and Byram*

for my Sensing students; they know exactly what to do. Yet there is enough connection-making potential for my iNtuitive students, who choose their ten events because of the intriguing connections. My Thinking students can rely on official documents for their information while my Feeling students will rely on people resources. All in all, my students are engaged and, as a class, we can have a rich discussion about that particular period in history.

I provide time for Extraverts to discuss their ideas and think aloud, but I also provide quiet time (I) through journals and reflective tasks. I provide hands-on experiences and give specific directions (S), but I also affirm leaps of intuition (N). When students can function in the classroom according to their natural inclinations, all types of students can shine at different times.

Dealing with all personality types in my classroom requires three things. First, I must understand my type, and how my own inclinations effect my teaching strategies. I must understand how the needs and natural tendencies of all personality types may be interacting with my own type. Second, I must create a respectful atmosphere for all learners styles. Teaching students to understand themselves and value all types is part of creating a respectful atmosphere. Accepting innate differences gives the message that it's OK to be who you really are, instead of placing one type of student on a pedestal as the "right kind." Finally, I give directions and provide activities which offer flexibility, allowing students to approach learning with their type strengths. I don't adapt each and every assignment, but my overall instructional strategies include a comfortable range for all types. I do not make one narrow assignment. I do not treat all students alike for they are not alike.

The MBTI and MMTIC give educators a set of powerful lenses to see and understand student differences. All different types of people are needed in our world. A teacher's challenge is to understand and purposely plan for each type's learning style.

-∞-

[1] The Murphy-Meisgeier Type Indicator for Children (MMTIC) can be purchased by special education teachers, your school psychologist, and people with appropriate test interpretation coursework. Contact CAPT,

the Center for Applications of Psychological Type, 2720 N.W. 6th Street, Gainesville, FL 32609, 800-777-2278, or CPP, Consulting Psychologist Press, P.O. Box 60070, Palo Alto, CA 94306-1490, 800-624-1765. Their catalog has many type resources.

[2] These category labels are from p. 3, Meisgeier, Murphy and Meisgeier, *A Teacher's Guide to Type* (CPP: 1989), $6.50.

[3] "Shy folk may be shy of dopamine," *BrainMind Bullletin*, Nov. 1987, Vol 13, No. 2.

[4] Gordon Lawrence, *People Types and Tiger Stripes* (Center for Applications of Psychological Type: 1982), p. 42.

[5] Isabel Briggs Myers and Mary H. McCaulley, *Manual: A Guide to the Development and Use of the Myers-Briggs Type Indicator*. (Consulting Psychologists Press: 1986). p. 106.

[6] *Ibid.*, p. 116.

[7] Isabel Briggs Myers, *Gifts Differing*. (Consulting Psychologists Press: 1980), p. 151.

[8] A more detailed list can be found in Lions-Quest Skills for Adolescence, 800-446-2700, 537 Jones Rd., P.O. Box 566, Granville, OH 43023-0566.

[9] Carol Gilligan, *In A Different Voice* (Harvard University Press: 1982)

[10] More explanation of this concept is available in *The Developing Child* by Elizabeth Murphy (Consulting Psychologists Press: 1992), p. 131.

[11] The percentages of teacher and students in this section come from David Keirsey and Marilyn Bates, *Please Understand Me* (Prometheus Nemesis Books: 1978), p. 155.

[12] The percentages on school administrators come from *Gifts Differing*, p. 51.

[13] Elizabeth Murphy, "I Am A Good Teacher" (1987), available from Center for the Applications of Psychological Type for $6. 800-777-2278.

[14] Scoring key is available from CAPT for $18. The MMTIC and scoring key must be ordered by a qualified person who has taken university coursework in psychological test or a qualified MBTI person. In most schools the school psychologist, social worker or special ed. teacher qualify.

[15] Diane Farris, *Type Tales* (Consulting Psychologists Press: 1991), $15. Write 3803 E. Bayshore Road, Palo Alto, CA 94303.

Thinking About Their Thinking:
A Reflective Practice

The biology of developmental stages ... Plateaus and spurts ... Myelination ...Constructing meaning Higher order thinking skills ... ... Time factors ... Reflections on thinking.

A kindergartner on the first day of school looked at his teacher with confusion, "What bus takes me home?" The teacher responded, "Do you know which bus you came on?" "Oh yes," the child replied confidently, "The yellow one."

How does a child's innocent bus memory turn into abstract reasoning? How does the clink-clang of a small child's pots and pans' experiment turn into a sophisticated science fair project? What is happening inside the child's brain to create such changes?

Understanding the human brain's development and function is new. The index of a large 1971 book on developmental psychology made no reference to the brain. Researchers have learned more about the brain in the last fifteen years than in all previous centuries. Now educators, in the classroom and at home, can take clues from new research findings and plan appropriate brain stretching experiences at each stage of a child's development.

This chapter will deal with the biological determinants which control students' thinking. It will explain the links between Piaget's stages and the brain's process of myelination. It will also discuss the "construction" of information into meaningful patterns as well as question asking and factors of time.

Neurons are the brain's building blocks. A neuron consists of a cell body, the information receiving end called dendrites, and a sending end called the axon. It's like a hand with many fingers reaching out to connect with many other fingers. Cells communicate with each other by sending an electrical impulse from cell to cell. Repeated appropriate sensory stimulation causes dendrites (receiving) to grow closer to other cells' axons (sending). The space between cells is the synapse. The smaller the space between the cells, the easier it is for the chemical electrical impulse to "jump the synapse" thus communicating with adjoining cells. The growing closer together increases the efficiency of the jump and creates the biological equivalent of "learning".

Neuron paths are created in the brain as a new skill or habit is learned. A path in the woods is worn by walking over and over it. Once created, the path remains a long time even if it is rarely used. A neuron pathway also remains even if it's used little. Think, for example, of once when you learned another language or to play an instrument. It took you a long time to gain your skill. Let's assume your skill is a bit rusty from lack of use over a period of years. If you wanted to, you could regain that skill with greater speed and ease than learning it the first time. The skill is a bit rusty but the brain pathway remains despite the time lapse.

Habits are hard to "break" because there's a neurological tendency to do the same thing, to head down the same path. Putting up a brain detour sign doesn't work. Instead, to break a habit you must consciously stop on the path and redirect your brain to handle the stimulation in a new way. It takes significantly more work to change habits than to simply allow old thought patterns to continue.

When you were born you had more neurons than you do today. Neurons which did not receive appropriate sensory stimulation to create useful pathways eventually atrophied and died. It's more difficult for adults to learn really new skills because their brains need to reroute paths to gain new habits. Young children are not rerouting brain paths but rather "hooking up" new awaiting cells. Neurons are effectively connected into useable groups called "mind maps" or "consciousness committees".[1] Thus, when a child has learned the multiplication tables, she has created pathways and an established map or committee which processes the information.

"Appropriate sensory stimulation" is the important phrase in the last paragraph. You can stimulate an infant with beautiful charts explaining quantum wave/particle theory but cause no learning. I can explain factoring algebraic equations to a first grader, but the child will not learn it. The child's brain does not have the mind maps to connect the information to earlier learning. The stimulation wanders aimlessly through the brain finding no connection, no hook. People do not learn without connecting to previous experience. Biologically, neurons must link with other neuronal patterns to extend the patterns. Thinking is

"The most important thing in education is to make young people think for themselves."
— *Albert Schweitzer*

"There are perhaps about one hundred billion neurons, or nerve cells, in the brain, and in a single human brain the number of possible interactions between these cells is greater than the number of atoms in the universe."
— *Robert Ornstein*

based on a system of linking old to new, and establishing pathways.

Developmental stage theory helps us realize which mind maps a child has developed. It gives us the understanding to appropriately plan for stretching the child's thinking path a bit further. Learning must start with the blocks already built. By repeated exposure to similar experiences sets of new blocks and paths are created.

Myelination[2] is the chemical process which readies neurons to function effectively. Myelin is a fatty substance which coats a neuron's axon, the transmitting end of the neuron. Myelin acts much like the rubber coating around an electrical cord. Without the rubber coating, electricity will not travel effectively from the socket to my hair dryer. The electrical impulse is contained and directed by the rubber coating. In a similar way, the myelin coating on the axon contains and directs the neuron's chemical-electrical impulse.

The process of myelination is observable as the child matures. At birth the infant is myelinating basic brainstem functions which control her body. This process of myelination enables the baby to effectively use her arms and hands. In about a year the neurons controlling the legs and feet are fully myelinated, enabling walking. The brain continues to myelinate neurons for over 16 years, the prefrontal lobe, the site of rational thinking is the last area completed.

∞

Developmental stages were observed by Piaget, first in his own children, then validated across cultures. We now understand Piaget's stages to be the result of the biological process of myelination. Understanding these developmental stages is a necessary foundation for anyone working with children.

"Sensory-motor" is the first Piagetian stage. In the first two years of life the child learns to manipulate his physical body. The child learns that physical movements cause results. "If I put my arm here and do this, I turn over on my back. Wow!"

The child develops basic brainstem functions and feelings, such as the sense of hunger, sleep, hot/cold, and comfort. The child begins to connect her hungry cry to food becoming available. When she looks at father's face, she realizes she gets attention. Even the traditional peek-a-boo game contributes to brain growth. The child is learning object

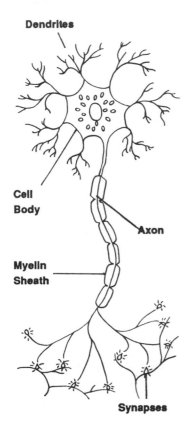

Dendrites

Cell Body

Axon

Myelin Sheath

Synapses

NEURON

permanence, "Mom is there before I cover up my eyes. She's gone when I close my eyes and reappears when I see again. Hmm . . . very interesting."

"Pre-operational" is the Piagetian second stage. This stage begins around two and usually continues until age eight.[3] The major task at this time is language acquisition. Infants across cultures begin language about the same time by making the same sounds. Yet each child ends up speaking the language of his culture.

During a child's third and fourth years, the neurons controlling the precise movements of the tongue and mouth are being myelinated. The child's auditory system has begun to be myelinated. This is the last system to become fully mature. At this stage children try out words they've heard without understanding the word's meaning. Homonyms thoroughly confuse them. "We are going to have chocolate mousse for dinner," can be unsettling. And, children are not ready for a true conversation. They often talk at others, rather than with others.

Language allows more elaborate thinking, but the lines between internal imagination and external reality have not yet been demarcated. Imagined friends and monsters are just as real to these children as other experiences. Their construct of time has not developed yet, causing their sense of past, present and future to be confused.

Compared to earlier ages, the child's attention span has increased, but it is very short in terms of traditional school tasks. Attention span, at all ages, is impacted by the amount already known and whether the individual cares about the subject. Kindergartners spend hours constructing a castle with blocks but little time with paper and pencil tasks.

Children at this stage can order objects by size and quantity but they do not "conserve" characteristics. A classic Piagetian task is illustrated when the child sees two identical glasses of milk then watches while one is poured into a thinner, taller glass and concludes that the taller glass has more milk. Objects which change in shape and size are not the same objects according to these developing minds. Counters spread out seem to be more than those piled closely. Quantity and size are confused.

To work on size and quantity "One Hundredth Day" celebrations are often held in our primary classrooms. For the hundredth day of school, children are asked to bring in 100 of something. One hundred paper clips and one hundred books are assembled. One hundred stuffed animals and one hundred pencils are on display. This provides the needed repeated experience with quantity, shape and size. Children discuss the 100s collections. They write and draw to internalize the concept. Rote memory or an adult explanation does not help the child's brain develop. Each child must develop these concepts for himself through repeated experiences. Children use art and imagination to internalize their experiences. Language is not the primary vehicle of learning for the younger child.[4] Most children are not ready to successfully handle the printed word and abstract meaning.

Children at this age are primarily tactile/kinesthetic and visual learners. To learn they need to move, touch, and experience their world first hand. The touching and moving systems have been myelinating since birth. Children's visual systems become fully myelinated after the first four months. These systems and the right hemisphere are fully operational before the auditory and left hemisphere systems.

Do boys or girls have the most difficulty learning to read? Boys, of course. But why? A number of contributing brain factors have been identified. First, boys have a higher prenatal level of testosterone. Testosterone has been found to delay the development of the left hemisphere.[5] In addition, the female brain has greater connection between hemispheres with more diverse language processing involving both hemispheres. The male brain is more specialized with its left hemisphere "almost exclusively set aside for the control of verbal abilities."[6] Finally, about 40% of the male's total body weight is muscle, compared to 23% for females.[7] The myelination process of muscle related neurons simply takes longer for males. There are more neurons relating to more muscle mass. While the male brain is still myelinating neurons for tactile/kinesthetic circuitry, the female brain has finished the motor connections and has begun to myelinate the language circuits.

∞

Plateaus and spurts in brain capabilities are a normal part of the brain growth cycle. Dr. Herman Epstein's research shows that "about 85 percent of children follow this schedule of (plateaus and spurts)".[8] During brain growth spurts neurons are being myelinated and effective pathways are formed. A period of lesser activity follows. This plateau allows new skills to be solidified and the pathway well worn. During plateaus it is important to refine earlier skills in order to have a strong foundation for the next growth spurt.[9] Plateau periods help thinking behaviors become automatic thus allowing the brain to focus energy on new tasks. When a student is struggling to remember 6x7 or 7x8, it is difficult for her to focus on the processes of long division. When the multiplication tables are fully memorized, the child's energy is free to master long division. The concept of plateaus and spurts is consistent with other body cycles like excursion and rest or wakefulness and sleep.

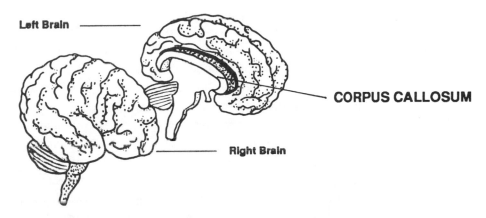

The corpus callosum is a bundle of nerve fibers which link the right and left hemispheres. The corpus callosum begins to be myelinated during the child's sixth or seventh year. This period is labelled "concrete operational" by Piaget. Experiences now "stick" because there are enough myelinated neurons and repeated experiences for children to build or "construct" concepts. Students become able to observe concrete changes and think about information.

Children at this stage are fascinated by discrepant scientific demonstrations. They know something is discrepant, or weird, but they don't have enough experience and abstract thought to understand an adult explanation. Students need real-life experiences to develop hypothesis. They need to do experiments, record data and draw conclusions.

During these years children continue to have a rich fantasy world. Heros and heroines are bigger than life. In the child's mind tremendous difficulties can be solved by simple magic. After all, since they have little understanding of how things really work, they see adults create magic daily. At this age children tend to have a blind admiration for older children, and are easily led. Friendships are important, but they haven't had enough interpersonal experience to effectively resolve interpersonal conflicts.

As always, the human brain requires a safe, caring environment to learn effectively. Threat causes "downshifting" to the Reptilian "fight or flight" thinking. Students in a threatening or understimulating environment have less opportunity to build appropriate neuron networks. The brain requires developmentally appropriate stimulation. Activities below the optimal stimulation bore and activities too far above optimal stimulation are wasted because the connecting supportive concepts are missing. Activities need to be "hard enough but not too hard."

Formal Operations is the final stage of brain myelination beginning around age ten and continuing until sixteen or later. Now the myelination process focuses on the frontal lobe in our foreheads. The frontal lobe is called the "executive brain". It analyzes, synthesizes and evaluates information. At this stage students begin to develop an "adult" thinking style. They are increasingly able to use information from interpersonal interactions, daily experiences, and classroom settings. They are beginning to think about information instead of just experiencing life. Students slowly become able to see information from more than one viewpoint. They can consider cause and effect relationships, and make their own conclusions. At the end of this growth the brain is fully myelinated and has the potential for adult thought processes.

> You have to question the accuracy and usefulness of IQ testing when you consider this observation from Renate Caine and Geoffrey Caine: "The removal of the prefrontal cortex results in no apparent change in IQ as we now measure it."

In the early teen years the brain's growth reaches a plateau, while the body's growth speeds up. Growth energy is needed for the development of the taller, larger sexually mature physical body. Even though the teen technically has the brain power to reason as an adult, he does not have experiences equal to adults and therefore is not likely to make "adult conclusions".

Stage theory gives educators general guidelines toward understanding children's behaviors. But remember stages are guidelines. Each child's brain has its own pattern and constructs mind maps in unique ways. Each child's progression through the stages depends on heredity, personality, perceptual modalities, environment, and family pressures. It is not reasonable to tell a child to grow four inches so she can play a better basketball game; she is not in conscious control of her height. Likewise, it is not reasonable to expect a student to control her brain's myelination process. The student is not responsible for her brain growth. Each child's brain growth is based on complex, biological imperatives and external stimulation.

Too often schools have expected students to function as small adults. It's not possible. As Healy says, "A fundamental truth about learning — you can lead the child to the problem, but you can't make the mental leap for her. She has to be ready, and she has to do it herself."[10] The stages of brain development, based on the myelination of neurons, are basic guidelines for educators to reflect on students' needs.

Being able to make "the mental leap" has to do with constructing meaning. This is a crucial process throughout the brain's growth stages. With the brain's developing capacity, students increase their ability to understand the relationship of events, actions and resulting consequences. This understanding is significantly different from memorization and regurgitation of facts. In our quickly changing world, knowing facts is not enough. I do not want my students to mimic others' thoughts. I want my students to learn to think for themselves.

"You cannot teach a man anything, you can only help him discover."
— *Galileo*

LEARNING AND BRAIN DEVELOPMENT
(The Spurts and Plateaus)

Age	Brain Area	Piaget	Myelin Growth
Birth	Right	sensory-motor	large motor visual system (fully at 3-4 months)
18/24 months	Left	pre-operational	language acquistion (vocal 3rd-4th year) (auditory 4th-5th year)
6/7 years	Left & Right	concrete operational	corpus callosum bridge
10+ years	Left & Right Frontal	formal operational	frontal lobes plan, decisions

The process of constructing meaning can be observed as my students work with five simple machines experiments: a board, marked off in ten centimeter units, resting on a triangular block and 100 gram to 2000 gram weights; pulleys on our door frame; an inclined plane and lego cars; and a series of toy gears.

First I want students to just "play around" with the materials. The play engages and stimulates their interest. My tactile/kinesthetic students get involved first. They are naturally attracted to manipulatives. For them it is a pleasant break from paper and pencil activities. Other students, usually the auditory ones, need to be steered to the manipulatives. Some seem to have an aversion to actually "doing". They seem perplexed, even frightened, at the idea of playing around with the materials. Are they uncomfortable due to their lack of experience with real things?

Children in our world today have less and less experience with real things. Some children never even play with blocks. In our age of electronic toys, sophisticated dolls, and TV, children are robbed of basic thought experiences which toys used to provide. The human brain still needs the richness of sensory experiences. Children need to observe and manipulate, to discuss and draw, in order to gain enough experience to abstractly "think". Without sensory experiences the brain has nothing to think about. Experiences are the base for the later developmental tasks of predicting, analyzing, and evaluating.

The simple machine experiments provide experiences for conceptual thinking. Adrienne plays with balancing the board on the triangular block (the fulcrum) using weights in different positions on the two ends. I challenge her to see if she can do it another way. After a few minutes she is successful. I challenge her to think again, "Adrienne, can you come up with six different ways?" I draw a model of the board and fulcrum, recording where she placed each weight with the gram values. She observes the relationship between her creation and my diagram. She continues to explore, and she records her arrangements.

As Adrienne began experimenting, I tried to be available immediately to applaud her efforts. Being an "extraverted feeler" she needs to tell me about her success and feel my approval. But now I want her to take another step: I want her to record her data. I conveniently make myself unavailable for her immediate gratification. "Adrienne, I need to work with Buddy, why not record your successes and I'll be back in a few minutes. Then you can explain it to me." I periodically glance at her. She's OK. She's working well. Later we'll discuss her findings. Then I'll challenge her to change the position of the board to off-center on the fulcrum and use the weights to again balance the board.

Eventually all students in my classroom play with the balance board. They are "playing" because there is still no specific assignment. I have merely encouraged the activity, yet this is the critical foundation for further thought. As students play I watch for opportune moments to interact with individuals or small groups of experimenters. As I expected, my intuitive students make generalizations after only a bit of experience, while my sensing students continue experimenting. They enjoy the experience without feeling a need to draw conclusions.

Finally, when all students have played around, I begin the first whole class discussion about the balance board. I start with Quadrant One, Anticipatory Set questions.[11] "Raise your hand if you were able to balance the board." Everyone's hand goes up because I delayed this discussion until I knew everyone had successfully played with the board. "Raise your hand if you can do it more than one way." Again all hands appear. "Good job!"

I ask students to draw different solutions on the chalkboard. "How are Erica's and Jack's solutions alike?" I wait, giving the Introverts time to compose their thoughts, then I probe for multiple ideas. My Extraverted hand-wavers have trouble waiting. I continue, "Can you predict how we can change just one weight and keep the board balanced?" (The solution is to move the board off center.) The first question about Erica's and Jack's solutions focused on classifying information. The second question stretches their thinking to predicting and analyzing information. It is more abstract. "In your cooperative TEAM's, come up with two ways you think will work." There is a buzzing of brains across the room combining their ideas for greater success.

The whole group reviews TEAM suggestions then I ask, "What name shall we call this triangular block?" Jon suggests, the "rested on". I introduce the term fulcrum and a visual image as a mnemonic aide, "Maybe the triangle is solid because it is full of crumbs. It is a ful-crum."

I go on with the assignment, "This week you may work alone or with a friend. Your task is to draw five diagrams of the weirdest, most far-out ways you can balance the board on the fulcrum. Try to come up with a way no one else has thought of. Then make one false diagram. Make the diagram look like it will work, but it really doesn't. Mix the false one in with your balancing diagrams and we will try to figure out which one doesn't really work. There is a second part to the assignment. Make a list of all of the things that have a fulcrum. A teeter-totter is an example, but fulcrums are used in many other ways. A lot of tools and machines use this idea."

This assignment is very different than a "read the textbook and do the worksheet on fulcrums and levers". First the challenge of making a wrong diagram is intriguing. It is the discrepant event which fascinates the brain. The brain ignores normal stimuli, focusing instead on the discrepant events in an attempt to reestablish normalcy. (In the same way the biological body strives to maintain homeostasis.) My students will apply what they already know, evaluate their new solutions then relate fulcrums to real-life examples. Later they will exchange diagram papers, identify the false balances and discuss the reasons. I will bring in a collection of simple devices — hammers, scissors, pliers, and pictures of the uses of this concept in complicated machinery using books such as David Macaulay's *The Way Things Work*.[12]

My students engage in similar processes with the inclined plane, gears, and pulleys. The concepts with each simple machine are different. It takes time to develop both my students' experiential background and their thinking. Yet in six weeks I have provided hands-on, real experiences which help my students' construct an internal understanding of the concepts. I have done only a little direct teaching, but my students have done a lot of "constructive learning". It has been a meaningful and fun learning experience.

Learning the order of our world is a natural outcome of appropriate experiences. Jacqueline Brooks from Columbia University, Teachers College explains it this way, "Constructivism reminds us that order exists only in the minds of people, so when we as teachers impose our order on students, we rob them of the opportunity to create knowledge and understanding themselves. Our task, then, is to understand and nurture the learning and development of our students. We must not do for them what they can, and must, do for themselves."[13]

Other opportunities to construct meaning abound in our school.

Through student council elections students construct a concept of community decision-making. Lobbying the zoning commission about a variance for a playground fence constructs meaning. Simulation games give realistic experiences and enable students to construct important concepts.[14] Math manipulatives help students construct the concept of our base ten system or experience what division represents.

My basic teaching techniques remain the same regardless of topic. I listen carefully to students' verbalization of their thinking and then, without criticism, give students experiences to stretch their thinking.

-∞-

Higher-Order Thinking Skills or HOTS was developed by Stanley Pogrow of the University of Arizona. It is a nationally validated program designed to help students construct concepts. It particularly targets "at-risk" students and has produced significant gains in reading and math even though the program doesn't teach reading or math. HOTS uses interesting, developmentally appropriate computer programs to stimulate student discussion. Teachers are trained to listen for the student's patterns of thinking and ask probing questions, "Why do you think it's true?" "Can you tell me more?" HOTS helps students to think about their own thinking strategies. (This process is known as "metacognition" by academicians.)

I am not a HOTS trained teacher, but I know my students who participate in our HOTS program have gained significant confidence in thinking. They have improved on generalizing concepts, making inferences, and applying ideas to new situations. Recently as I was helping Adrienne work on a problem she captured the essence of her HOTS experience when she said, "Launa, I don't want you to explain it. Ask me questions like in HOTS." I laughed, caught my breath and figured out a good question.

I tend to be skeptical that any prepackaged program can meet the needs of a broad group of students because I know how much I constantly adjust my strategies to create an appropriate learning environment. However the HOTS program does develop language and thought patterns. It teaches students to link information, analyze what is happening and verbalize their thoughts. The HOTS program does the job. I see the results in my students and also in HOTS' expanding research database.[15]

Jane Healy, writing in *Endangered Minds: Why Our Children Don't Think*, documents our children's increasing lack of significant language thinking experiences.[16] She cites Dr. Bambi Schieffelin of the Department of Anthropology at NYU, who "like many others, is concerned that children are not receiving large enough daily doses of talk either at home or at school."[17] Dr. Catherine Snow from Harvard agrees the quality of conversation children have with adults is extremely important and too often lacking. "In those precious times together at the dinner table, for example, parents who take the time to discuss topics thoughtfully, who talk about events and ideas, are helping their children become much better thinkers than those who focus more on the food or the situation at hand."[18]

For an increasing number of children, across all socioeconomic lines, TV has become a major purveyor and source of language. TV language does not provide the in-depth thinking experiences children need to develop. A Florida university teacher observes this problem, "It's a source of amazement to me how many students can't link ideas together; they can't follow one idea logically with another . . . they have such poor verbal skills. If you don't have a grasp of the language you have no tools to work with. You haven't formed the appropriate categories verbally to combine ideas. Language changes the way your brain sets up the categories it works with."[19]

∞

A final factor in quality thinking is the matter of **when** we do it. The Dunns point up the importance of understanding how daily energy patterns effect learning. I can observe energy peaks in my students. Thorin is never alert at our morning meeting. Anna plops down in the reading corner around 1:00, tired from earlier activities. When my students mentor the kindergartners, the differing energy levels of the younger children are obvious. Educational systems which really strive for each child's success must take body rhythms into account.

Ted Sizer raises another thought provoking time issue.[20] Suppose you, a competent adult, are about to start a new job. At nine AM your boss explains that you are to sit in this desk, do this work and not talk to anyone else. When it's ten o'clock you are to go to the third floor. There you will have a new boss. He will assign you a desk, you are to do the work he gives you, and again do not talk to anyone else. At eleven you will report to your third boss, at twelve you will work for your fourth boss, at one PM your boss will be ... , at two your boss .... As a competent adult would you really be able to get much work done, much less find it a satisfying process? Children are less resilient than adults. Switching bosses according to a timed schedule is a daily, "normal" experience for students, but it is not normal for their brains.

My students spend about two hours daily in "work time". Mike tends to stick to one subject saying, "Today I'll work on my report, and tomorrow I'll concentrate on math." Justin prefers to work a while on one thing, and then a bit on another. Both boys are making their own choices based on their own styles. Both do a good job and finish their work effectively.

A third time issue is "time on task." Teachers hear a lot of rhetoric about "time on task," essentially meaning students are concentrating. But concentration without pause is not the natural brain cycle. Study skill programs designed for middle school students recommend a rhythm of quality concentration interspersed with breaks.[21] This "off-task time" provides time for incubation of ideas, and refreshes the body. Our brains' natural rhythm of approximately 90 minute cycles[22] continues during sleep and wakefulness. Continual concentration is exhausting. In my classroom I expect students to flow in and out of concentration. They work and take breaks as needed. I plan for this natural flow by providing a variety of activities like the simple machine experiments and math

> "Learners need time to allow for new connections to be made. They need "space" for reflection."
> — *Caine and Caine*

puzzles. Students don't think of these as work. They think these materials are for "breaks".

Observing students' thinking patterns is an important task for a reflective teacher. As I learned to "see" a student's thinking pattern, I became more effective in planning the experiences which would lead that child to learn with greater success and satisfaction. As students' growth stages became visible to me, I was more able to stretch and stimulate each child's learning. The curriculum materials I use become the vehicles that stimulate student thinking. This thinking quite literally engages new neuron dendrites and creates new pathways. As I understood the brain's myelination process, I grew to respect students' plateaus and spurts and I had a better sense of when to push and when to back off. When I have taught long division with the best multi-sensory methods and my student still doesn't understand it, I back off. The child's brain isn't ready. I'm comfortable waiting and trying again in a couple of months. Understanding the biological building blocks of thinking is a crucial part of my expertise as an effective educator. This base enables me to help each child learn with success.

-∞-

[1] The term "mind maps" is used in Israel Rosenfield's *The Invention of Memory* (Basic Books: 1988), "consciousness committees" was coined by William Calvin in *The Cerebral Symphony* (Bantam Books: 1990).

[2] For a non-technical discussion of myelination see Jane Healy's *Your Child's Growing Mind* (Doubleday: 1987).

[3] Jane Holmes, The Children's Hospital, Boston (Presentation handout), "The Brain from A to Y." Sponsored by the California Neuropsychology Services, Minneapolis, April 25, 1987.

[4] Healy, *Your Child's Growing Mind*, has an excellent chapter on "Unfolding Language".

[5] Bloom, Lazerson and Hofstadter, *Brain, Mind and Behavior* (Educational Broadcasting Corporation: 1985), p. 227.

[6] Anne Moir and David Jessel, *BrainSex* (Mandarin: 1989), p. 43.

[7] Diane McGuinness, *When Children Don't Learn* (Basic Books: 1985), p. 85.

[8] Healy, p. 86.

[9] Epstein, in *The 4Mat System: Teaching to Learning Styles with Right/ Left Mode Techniques* by Bernice McCarthy (EXCEL, Inc.: 1980), p. 64.

[10] Healy, p. 62.

[11] Please refer to the chapter on Learning Styles for more information.

[12] David Macaulay, *The Way Things Work* (Houghton Mifflin: 1988).

[13] Jacqueline Grennon Brooks, "Teachers and Students: Constructivists Forging New Connections," *Educational Leadership*, February 1990.

[14] Interact is a reliable company for teacher created simulation games, P.O. Box 997-491, Lakeside, CA 92040.

[15] For more information call the HOTS headquarters at Tucson, AZ (602-621-1305).

[16] Jane Healy, *Endangered Minds: Why Our Children Don't Think* (Simon and Schuster: 1990).

[17] *Ibid.*, p. 90.

[18] *Ibid.*, p. 91.

[19] *Ibid.*, p. 100.

[20] Contact the Coalition of Essential Schools, Box 1938, Brown University, Providence, RI 02912.

[21] *Practical Intelligence for Schools*, Yale University, Dept. of Psychology, Box 11A, Yale Station, New Haven, CT 06520-7447.

[22] *PragMagic*, by Marilyn Ferguson, Pat Perrin, and Wim Coleman, (Simon & Schuster Pocket Books: 1990), pp. 45, 53.

Intelligence: Broader and More Inclusive

6

IQ ... Gardner's theory of multiple intelligence — linguistic, logical-mathematical, visual-spatial, musical-rhythmic, bodily-kinesthetic, interpersonal and intrapersonal.

What is intelligence? What are the implications for schools?

Around the turn of the century Alfred Binet and physician Theophile Simon were asked by the French government to develop a test which would identify "retarded" children so these children could be given special help. Their test was published in 1905. Over time this test came to be used to predict academic performance rather than to identify children with special needs.

In the United States a Stanford University professor made an English version which continues to be used today, the Stanford Binet IQ Test. In these early years IQ was believed to be an inherited trait.

In the 1930's another psychologist decided to do an intelligence experiment. He removed two little girls from a dreary orphanage and put them with a group of retarded women "who gave them massive stimulation and attention."[1] The girls' IQ scores changed from below 50 to near normal. This was the first documented evidence that IQ's are affected by the stimulation a child receives.

In the 1960's J.P. Guilford broadened the concept of a single intelligence by identifying 120 factors affecting intellectual ability. His work, the Structure of Intellect or SOI, continues to be used by many schools. The SOI test evaluates twenty-six different thinking abilities. School districts often use it as a screening test to identify students for both gifted and special help programs[2]

In the past ten years Marian Diamond and colleagues, neuroanatomists at Berkeley University, have published significant research on their experiments to improve the intelligence of rats. From their research it is clear that rats in enriched environments develop structural changes in their brains. The enriched rat environment consists of "play groups of ten to twelve rats, in a large, well-lit, multi-leveled cage filled with swings, slides, ladders, bridges, an assortment of toys, frequently changing stimuli, and a variety of challenges."[3] Diamond believes these experiments have significant implications for the education of children. Do classrooms provide enough changing stimuli, challenges, and opportunities to communicate with others?

In 1983 Howard Gardner of Harvard University further expanded the theories of intelligence when he published *Frames of Mind: The Theory of Multiple Intelligences*.[4] Gardner established a background for the biological and cross-cultural foundations of intelligence. He identified seven distinct types of intelligence: *linguistic, logical-mathematical, visual-spatial, musical-rhythmic, bodily-kinesthetic, interpersonal* and *intrapersonal*. Cross-cultural studies show these intelligences are valued differently in different societies. Five of the intelligences are relevant to "the Arts". In the United States some intelligences are valued more than others, yet any society needs contributions from all seven intelligences in order to thrive.

Thomas Armstrong is a former special education teacher who translated Gardner's academic theory into practical examples for our classrooms.[5] He writes vivid descriptions of elementary students using all of Gardner's intelligences. His book describes methods to teach basic skills to all students by using all of the seven intelligences.

David Lazear, in *Seven Ways of Knowing and Seven Ways of Teaching*,[6] encourages us to teach **about** the seven intelligences, teach **for** all intelligences as subjects, and teach **with** multiple intelligences.

In my classroom a conceptual map of the seven intelligences is posted on our bulletin board. I teach about each intelligence and use all intelligences in the process of teaching.

Linguistically intelligent students are easy to spot in our classroom. They thrive on reading books or writing copiously. Anything which involves language engages these students. School is often very enjoyable because the academic expectations complement their natural linguistic intellect.

Flora is a fourth grader in our classroom who displays linguistic intelligence. This year she did a project on the King Arthur stories. Her

"We are all so different largely because we all have different combinations of intelligences. If we recognize this, I think we will have at least a better chance of dealing appropriately with the many problems that we face in the world."

— Howard Gardner

interest began as she read *The Mists of Avalon* (an adult book requiring a high level of reading skill). Then Flora researched other King Arthur stories to compare and contrast characters' traits.

Kristy, a fifth grader, also displays this linguistic intelligence. Her writing skills are excellent; she is writing a novel. On different weeks as I would assign writing projects to focus on particular skills, Kristy would invariably come to me and ask if the next chapter of her book would fulfill the assignment instead of writing something else. She consistently incorporated the skills I targeted into her next chapter in order to prove she understood that writing technique.

Logical-mathematical intelligence has significant respect in our society. Our world of computers and high-tech industry has boosted this intelligence to a top national priority. This intelligence is not the simplistic ability to do mathematical computation. It is the abstract thinking of engineers. It is the manipulation of patterns and relationships. It is the function of variables and analogies.

Two of my sixth graders, Morgan and Thorin, have outstanding logical-mathematical intelligence. They see patterns and relationships in everything. Chess, word games and number concepts are all their forte. They love to create and debate the correctness of solutions to logical puzzles. They have a clear understanding of high school algebra.

Our national math standards focus on logical-mathematical thinking. These standards encourage increased use of calculators and computers in our classrooms, freeing students to think mathematically rather than just computing numbers. In my classroom I stimulate this intelligence with games such as "24", logic puzzles, visual-spatial activities such as Tangrams and the Tower of Hanoi, science experiments, inventor's fairs and Future Problem Solving strategies.

Visual-Spatial intelligence, processed by the right hemisphere, includes the realm of geometry and the visual arts of sculpting, drawing, and painting.

Elliot Eisner explains his rationale for visual-spatial thinking and art education. "Art is perhaps humanity's most essential, most universal language. It is not a frill, but a necessary part of communication. Indeed, the quality of civilization can be measured by the breadth of the symbols used. We need words, music, dance and the visual arts to give expression to the profound urgings of the human spirit."[7]

Spatially intelligent people tend to think in pictures and images. Thinking in images is reported by Einstein, as he visualized riding on a beam of light, and Kekulé, as he visualized the benzene ring. It is evident in the work of Leonardo da Vinci and Buckminster Fuller and the gifts of Van Gogh or Picasso.

This intelligence also includes the understanding of three-dimensional space and two-dimensional representations. It involves mental skills to rotate objects and the mental acuity to internalize size and shape. These skills are important to engineers, pilots, architects and designers, as well as artists.[8]

In my classroom excellent visual-spatial skills are evident when Patrick enlarges and vertically distorts the face of a comic character. It is evident as I watch Morgan teaching other children origami. It is evident in Anna's delicate watercolors as she expresses her mood and in Thorin's 3-D alphabet embedded within another picture. It is also evident in Erin's visual-spatial memory which was an important factor in achieving her national third place chess rank.

There are many ways to stimulate and develop this intelligence. I always have art materials available for student use. Drawings are a regular feature in my students' journals. Drawing activities help students to "see" with greater clarity.[9] Each week I incorporate a visual arts project along with our paper/pencil assignments. Our math activities include tangrams and pentagrams. Creative geo-block designs are built for other students to replicate. Tessellations are designed. Students have maze-making contests. I use mind mapping and guided imagery to develop visual-spatial thinking.

Musical-rhythmic intelligence, has been valued by cultures throughout history, but it often is only given lip-service in schools. Music engages both hemispheres. Lyrics are processed by the left hemisphere, and the melodic tone is processed by the right.[10]

The cerebellum is responsible for the "programs" of movement. It controls muscle tone and the body's positions. The programs fire off as we walk or engage in a thousand routine movements. These programs are critical for the musician. As I practice my violin I am creating neuronal pathways to string together a program which eventually allows me to bow and finger simultaneously. This program takes conscious thought to begin with. However, after hours and hours of practice a pathway is

"Pablo Picasso resisted school stubbornly and seemed completely unable to read or write. The other students grew used to seeing him come late with his pet pigeon — and with his paintbrush he always carried as if it were an extension of his own body."
— *Mildred Goertzel, Picasso's tutor*

"Musical training is a more potent instrument than any other, because rhythm and harmony find their way into the inward places of the soul."
— *Plato*

created. This repeated practice is similar to a small child needing months to learn to feed himself. Professional musicians, like Olympic champions, have finely tuned their cerebellums to turn complex routines into automatic performances.

Some authorities believe musical intelligence precedes linguistic intelligence. Studies of infants show a very early response to music. In less technological societies everyone is expected to make music and expert music makers are highly honored.

Alexa joined our classroom this year. She is musically brilliant by my standards. She takes private violin lessons and is unbelievably great. She tells me how hard it is to learn certain pieces, but she plays as though she is entertaining the Queen. Over the years I've been impressed with students who could play the piano with grace and expertise. Now I internally know how it feels to see a nine year old play the violin better than I may ever play it. Alexa is wonderful and I am learning slowly.

Many students receive inadequate stimulation, or none at all, for their musical intelligence, since music and art are often the first cuts made into tight school budgets. In 1986-87 "there were only 23 full-time teachers of the arts at the elementary level for the (Chicago) system's 498 elementary schools."[11] "Similar declines have struck arts programs in Boston, Philadelphia, Los Angeles, and other cities. In California, there is now [1989] only one music teacher for every 1,600 students."[12] Some parents, of course, are able to pay for music lessons outside our public school system, but shouldn't all students be encouraged to develop this basic intelligence?

Music and rhythm are used extensively in accelerated learning and super-learning classrooms. In the same mode I use music for background, as a relaxation aide, for transitions, and during journal writing.[13] I ask students to make up multiplication raps, and put geographic information to rhythms. My student council members have created songs about our school's behavioral expectations. Children created a fundraiser jingle by rewriting words of a familiar tune. An assembly uses music to honor Martin Luther King, Jr. Our students write original operettas around our school theme. All children in my class are not musically gifted but all should have the opportunity to develop the musical intelligence which enriches our lives and aids our memory.

Bodily-kinesthetic intelligence garners a great deal of respect in certain select fields, but in many schools the kinesthetic learner is valued little. On one hand athletes have been valued in every culture since before the Greeks. Sports figures are paid enormous salaries for their expertise. On the other hand dancers, bricklayers and carpenters are compensated with much lower salaries. Many skilled workers rely on their bodily-kinesthetic intelligence. These people keep our airplanes in the sky, household machines functioning, and our cars running efficiently, yet gain little prestige for their expertise.

In my classroom the bodily-kinesthetic children are our actors, our mimics and our movers. These children thoroughly enjoy manipulating math and science materials. They create experiments and build with legos and gears. They like to weave and work with wood. They obtain the respect of their peers as they perform plays, and during physical education classes or recess.

Gardner's last two categories are personal intelligences. *Intrapersonal intelligence* denotes the ability to understand and manage oneself. These people have a deep sense of who they are, the intense understanding of self that sets them apart from others.

I use a number of self evaluation techniques to help children develop their Intrapersonal intelligence. Often I ask, "Scale of 1 to 5, how far are you on your (report ... math ... writing ...)?" Students put up the number of fingers that represent their evaluation. "Scale of 1 to 5, how did you like the historical video on Martin Luther King, Jr.?" This quick technique helps children think about their feelings and evaluate their progress. Periodically, I give students self-evaluation forms which relate to their own goals, our behavior expectations or our school's theme.

Intrapersonal intelligence is also promoted by journal work. During our journal time I expect students to write and draw for half an hour. Some students have the technical skills to write but feel they have nothing to say. Knowing your own ideas is an important growth step for some students.

Teaching students about their learning styles also fosters this intelligence. Allowing students the freedom to make decisions, take responsibility and organize their own time fosters Intrapersonal intelligence. Many of Rich's ten *MegaSkills*[14] reflect this intelligence.

Interpersonal intelligence is expertise in understanding other people.

"From many years of observation I have found that I have rarely met a stupid child, but I have met many stupid and debilitating, and yes, even brain-damaging systems of education. As we subsequently discovered, a child can learn math as a rhythmic dance and learn it well ... He can learn almost anything and pass the standard test if he is dancing, tasting, touching, hearing, seeing, and feeling information. He can delight in doing so because he is using much more of his mind-brain-body system than conventional teaching generally permits. So much of the failure in school comes directly out of boredom, which itself comes directly out of the larger failure to stimulate all those areas in the child's brain which could give him so many more ways of responding to his world."

— *Jean Houston*

This is a special understanding of the emotions and concerns of others. Often these people are the Feeling personality type. They are natural leaders and natural organizers of groups and they tend to choose counseling and leadership occupations where their people skills are utilized. When combined with a highly developed linguistic intelligence, these people can exhibit great charisma.

Experiences which promote interaction with other people, and reflection on how people behave fosters Interpersonal intelligence. Our school teaches social skills to foster Interpersonal intelligence. Cooperative TEAM activities, service-learning projects, Student Council committees, or group projects also develop this intelligence.

Every child possesses all of the seven intelligences to some degree. Some excel in more than one of them. In my classroom I strive to value all of these intellectual processes by specifically planning opportunities to involve my students in all of them.

∞

Our concept of intelligence is changing. It is no longer acceptable to value only a narrow range of abilities. We have become aware of the importance of valuing many diverse ways of being smart.

In his most recent book, *Multiple Intelligences: The Theory in Practice*, Howard Gardner challenges many assumptions about the role and practices of schools.[15]

"In my view, the purpose of school should be to develop intelligences and to help people reach vocational and avocational goals that are appropriate to their particular spectrum of intelligences. People who are helped to do so, I believe, feel more engaged and competent and therefore more inclined to serve the society in a constructive way."[16]

In later pages, Gardner further develops this theme. "My belief in the importance — indeed, the necessity — of individual-centered education derives from two separate but interlocking propositions First of all it has now been established quite convincingly that individuals have quite different minds from one another. Education ought to be so sculpted that it remains responsive to these differences. Instead of ignoring them, and pretending that all individuals have (or ought to have) the same kinds of minds, we should instead try to ensure that everyone receive an education that maximizes his or her own intellectual potential.

"The second proposition is equally compelling. It may once have been true that a dedicated individual could master the world's extant knowledge or at least some significant part of it. So long as this was a tenable goal, it made some sense to offer a uniform curriculum. Now, however, no individual can master even a single body of knowledge completely, let alone the range of disciplines and competencies."[17]

∞

One of my colleagues at the Clara Barton School, Sonja Walker, wrote this delightful song for use in her class. She describes it as a whole language, whole brain, start-the-day-in-group-meeting (interpersonal) lesson using music, pictures, movement and language to help first, second and third grade students understand (intrapersonal) the many ways for them to learn. Sonja suggests that a teacher leading this song, and the students too, can act out the ideas as they sing. Possible gestures to go along with each line are suggested here by the "Peanut People" drawings of an eleven year old student.

A Celebration of Intelligences (Tune: *Do, Re, Mi* from *The Sound of Music*)

1. *Intrapersonal*		Know myself and how I grow
2. *Bodily/Kinesthetic*		My whole body helps me think
3. *Logical/Mathematical*		Puzzles, patterns, problem-solve
4. *Verbal/Linguistic*		Words and language make a link
5. *Rhythmic/Musical*		Sounds and music fill my brain
6. *Visual/Spatial*		Shapes and pictures make it plain
7. *Interpersonal*		Other people help me grow

And that brings me back to

Know, Know, Know ....

[1] James McConnell, *Understanding Human Behavior* (Holt, Rinehart and Winston: 1986), p. 555.

[2] SOI Institute,343 Richmond Street, El Segundo, CA 90245 (213) 322-5532. The basic book is J.P. Guilford's *Way Beyond the IQ* (Creative Education Foundation: 1977).

[3] Michael Hutchison, *Megabrain* (Beech Tree Books: 1986), p. 36.

[4] Howard Gardner, *Frames of Minds: the Theory of Multiple Intelligences* (Basic Books: 1983). See also Howard Gardner's most recent book on intelligence, *Multiple Intelligences: The Theory in Practice* (Harper Collins: 1993).

[5] Thomas Armstrong, *In Their Own Way*. (Tarcher: 1987), also the more recent work, *Seven Kinds of Smart*, (Penguin: 1993).

[6] David Lazear, *Seven Ways of Knowing* (Skylight Publishing: 1991), and *Seven Ways of Teaching* (Skylight: 1991).

[7] Ernest L. Boyer, "Art as Language: Its Place in the Schools," *Beyond Creating: The Place for Art in America's Schools* (A Report by the Getty Center for Education in the Arts: 1985).

[8] *Thinking Visually* by Robert McKim was created to train people for these occupations. The book has a wealth of experiences in all areas of visual thinking. (Lifetime Learning Publications: 1980).

[9] For teachers without visual art training I'd suggest using Mona Brookes' *Drawing with Children* (Tarcher: 1986) or Betty Edwards' *Drawing on the Artist Within* (Simon and Schuster: 1986).

[10] Gardner, p. 118.

[11] Charles Fowler, "The Arts Are Essential to Education," *Educational Leadership*, November 1989, p. 61.

[12] *Ibid.*

[13] I use a wide variety of instumental music to help students be aware of different sound patterns including Baroque, Native American flutes, and calming synthesized music. If you are buying your first tape for your classroom I'd suggest "Optimalearning Baroque" available from Learning Forum. (Call 800-527-5321 for a catalogue, and remember to make a copy of the music to take to school. Tapes in classrooms can become damaged, so keep the orginal at home.)

[14] Dorothy Rich, *MegaSkills* (Houghton Mifflin: 1988).

[15] Howard Gardner, *Multiple Intelligences: The Theory in Practice*, (Harper Collins: 1993).

[16] *Ibid.*, p. 9.

[17] *Ibid.*, p. 71.

Changing Lives:
Children in My Classroom

Stories of children and their needs—Jonathan ... Sarah ... Leah ... Chue ... Morgan ...
Margaret ... Erin ... Patrick ... But no single recipe.

The children in my classroom are special, just as all children are special in every classroom across the country. Each child is unique, having particular strengths and difficulties. Schools have no purpose unless the children grow. As an educator I must do whatever necessary to see they are successful.

This chapter focuses on some of the children I have worked with in the last two years. They span fourth through seventh grades. The children discussed are African American, Native American, Southeast Asian, and Caucasian. Forty-two percent of our students are people of color, but I have chosen not to link a child's racial-ethnic group to my descriptions in this chapter. The children's diverse cultural experience adds to the richness of my classroom.

∞

Jonathan came into my classroom as a large, overweight, withdrawn fifth grader. He was reading at a first grade level. When I could get him to write, he printed awkwardly. He had nothing to say on paper, nothing to draw and nothing to write. He made mistakes with even the simplest subtraction. He had little experience with childhood games, or exposure to typical boyish sports. He hadn't played football, softball, or basketball. He threatened other children with his mannerisms and his size.

The first year I made very slow, very tentative progress with Jonathan. His home environment had been disruptive. I needed to gain his trust. I needed to convince him that he could learn. I needed to convince him that school was worth his effort. He couldn't do many assignments simply because he didn't have the skills or the background. I adjusted and readjusted expectations to his level. He worked slowly without really engaging his brain. I needed to be aware of him at all times. It felt like he was a time bomb, about to explode.

Over the summer the school was notified that he had enrolled in another school, but to my surprise Jonathan showed up the first day. We started this second year together tentatively. But Jonathan cooperated better. Gradually Jon became able to make school progress. He began taking his spelling words home. One Friday he surprised himself by achieving a perfect score. Twenty correct spelling words at a fifth grade level was a tremendous achievement for this sixth grader. The previous year he didn't learn ten words on the third grade level.

During our October mini-courses, I taught a volleyball class. Jonathan chose to be with me. His size was an advantage, but he had never played the game before. He learned the basic skills and improved. But, most importantly, he started laughing. He was cooperating and he was having fun.

As a sixth grader, Jon was reading at a primer level. No other students were quite as limited so I could not place him in an instructional group. If Jon was going to learn to read I would need to spend some time with him in a one-to-one relationship. I squeezed in as much time as possible. I selected a few books at Jon's level and asked him to pick the one he wanted to read. Choice is a very important factor when facing a difficult situation. I read a paragraph; he read the same paragraph back to me. When he stumbled I reread the same paragraph — without commenting on his mistakes — and asked him to read it again. I wanted Jonathan to feel successful and fluent. I wanted Jon to feel books had value for him.

January arrived and our student council sponsored a used book fair. The first day Jonathan surprised me. "Launa, do you want to see the books I bought?" A smile swept across my face, "I sure do!" He had bought an Adams family book and a book about basketball stars. I rejoiced. In the past year and a half I had often wondered if he would ever value books.

In February Jon was able to be an effective "book group" member.

He and three other students read *How to Eat Fried Worms*, and put on a play. He was a sixth grader reading a third grade book, but I was delighted. He had improved enough to work with other children! Yes, he had a long way to go, but he was unstuck, engaged. He had a chance to become a reader now.

Last year Jon could not subtract large numbers. This January he surprised me with his ease in learning to measure the degrees in an angle and enlarge three-dimensional geometric shapes. He ended up teaching other students how to do it. This March, when he was successfully subtracting fractions with uncommon denominators and multiplying fractions, I sent out the word for other adults in the building to stop Jon in the halls and congratulate him on his significant math achievements.

Jonathan has come out of his withdrawn tightness; now he constantly tests the system. This behavior is quite typical. Children who missed appropriate developmental experiences need to learn all the socialization they lack. Often their behavior, when more confident, swings too far. They need some time to find the center. Jon teases. He tries to get by without working "hard enough but not too hard." Yet he's figured out that he can get extra privileges when he behaves. That's an important step! His life had been so confusing that he wasn't connecting the relationship between what he did and what happened to him.

I still need to be aware of Jonathan at all times, but I'm pleased. He still has behavioral problems when I have a substitute teacher, but I believe he will become able to improve that also. The stable and caring classroom environment has promoted healing in Jon. He is making progress. As the feelings and relationships heal (the Reptilian safety and emotional Limbic centers), his academic work has a chance for success. He has begun to taste success and will never be the same again.

-∞-

When Sarah first arrived, a few weeks into the school year, I was very concerned. Her file, from her previous school, came with a note — "Call Us." Her first classroom writing told the story of her father beating her mother and being jailed, repeatedly. It was full of anger and fear. She hated her father and wanted him dead.

A few weeks later, our lessons took us to a nature area. After the nature program, we had 15 minutes before returning to school. I

"The single most important thing in education is for each person to find at least one thing he or she connects to, gets excited by, feels motivated to spend more time with."

— *Howard Gardner*

encouraged my students to play and run off some of their energy. I thought Sarah had made friends but she clung close to me. She was dressed inappropriately, a fourth grader in little heels which dug into the grassy hill. She couldn't run in her shoes but I encouraged her to roll down the hill with others. She clung. I asked her what she did with her friends at home. She replied, "I don't." "You don't play with friends at home? What do you like to do?" "I like to do my chores." Clearly this fourth grader was not experiencing a typical childhood.

At the end of February, Sarah was to move to Nebraska. On her last day I began with relaxation and a guided imagery with our whole class. "Close your eyes and imagine that this is your last day at our school. This weekend you will drive to Nebraska. You will drive for hours and hours, into a new state and a new life. Feel the trip in your imagination. Imagine looking out of the window as you travel down the road, away from all you already know to a new place ... Now imagine walking up the steps of your new school with your mother. Notice how your stomach feels ... Imagine the school, the new teacher and the new classroom ... Think about how you feel as you walk in the door ... When you really understand your feelings open your eyes to our classroom."

Sarah was sitting next to me as we began the class discussion of our imaginary experience. "How did you feel going into the new school?" Sarah's classmates articulated what they felt, and thus validated what Sarah may have been feeling. Sarah's classmates put words to many typical concerns: apprehension, just plain scaredness, a sense that all the classmates already had friends, fear the teacher wouldn't like her ...

Next I both affirmed and prodded, "I believe Sarah has many strengths which will help her to deal with this change. Who can think of one strength that Sarah has?" The response was not instantaneous; as a new-to-school fourth grader Sarah had not been a leader. But, the response came. "Sarah, I'm sure you'll make friends easily because you are nice." "Sarah, I really like the way you helped me learn my spelling words. You are a friendly helper." "Sarah, I liked it when you were new and asked to join our jump rope game. You jumped really good." "I like the way you stand up for yourself. You stand up for yourself but you don't put other people down." Many children responded, verbalizing the strengths they saw in Sarah. I ended our session by asking Sarah what she knew about her next school.

"Children who have been hurried to grow up fast have many feelings, fears, angers, and anxieties that they are often unable to express."
— *David Elkind*

Another girl had organized a special party for Sarah in the social worker's office during recess. (Our social worker had spent significant time with Sarah in a "new students" group, and afterward as she recognized this child's background.) There was a buzz of activity, according to the social worker, with treats and gifts and happy hugs.

As the day closed, I gave Sarah her learning style folder and a personal letter to her next teacher. She gathered up her belongings, her portfolio containing her stories and accomplishments, her cards, a farewell poster, artwork and self-evaluations. We hugged and I remembered the child who I met just five months ago. She is better; she will never be that same child. Our classroom has made her stronger. I am thankful we were able to touch her life.

-∞-

Leah's head hung, her shoulders drooped. She was a shell of a child in fifth grade. In the past two years she had been absent more days of school than she had attended. Her mother had repeatedly been served with legal truancy papers. Obviously the frequent absences had caused academic weakness.

After lengthy discussions with our social worker, psychologist and special education teachers, we concluded that Leah seemed invisible to herself. She was languid. She wasn't engaged; she wasn't living her own life.

We enlisted the help of other adults in our school. I showed her picture to my team members, to our office staff, the lunchroom supervisor and engineers. My request was simple, "If you see this child, please greet her. Ask her how she is today or tell her you're glad to see her in school today."

Despite my efforts Leah continued to miss school. I conferred repeatedly with her mother, but Leah continued to be absent. One time she said she didn't have clean clothes so she couldn't come. I found some sweat shirts for her at an inexpensive recycled clothes store. Once, in the middle of our cold Minnesota winter, she came in shivering. She had on a damp sweat shirt and her bus had been late. Our school nurse found her something dry to wear. She didn't return for a week.

Leah was a perfectly bright girl, with the intelligence to go to college — if I could get her to school. We put her on a computer-dialed

"The successful schools we visited were true communities of learning and places where students were known and have ongoing contact with their teacher."
— *The Carnegie Foundation,*
"An Imperiled Generation" (1988)

morning wake-up call. It helped a little, but it wasn't the answer. In February I wrote a letter stating my tentative decision to retain her for another year. She simply had not done the fifth grade work. I don't believe retaining her would have helped, but I hoped the threat of retention might work. I gambled and it made an impact. Leah's attendance improved. She worked harder at school but she was playing catch-up.

I don't believe even this threat would have helped if our other strategies — adults speaking to her, engaging her — had not been in place. When the office needed help stapling, I asked Leah to do it. (Yes, even though she was terribly behind in her classwork.) When the lunch supervisor needed help, I sent Leah. The social worker came by weekly to take her out of class for a friendly chat. People were consciously working to engage her and help her feel valuable.

The last week of school the retention decision needed to be made. Would I allow Leah to continue on to the sixth grade? Leah and her mother met with me and the principal. I restated my belief that Leah was bright and capable, that she had the potential for college. I reviewed her small, but significant improvements in completing work and attendance. I purposely talked slowly and deliberately as I asked, "Leah, do you want to be successful, and go on to sixth grade? Will you come to school every day?" I got a commitment. Finally we agreed to allow Leah to go on, with the clear expectations of constant attendance and completed work. I held my breath over the summer and hoped for success.

In September I immediately set up Goal-Setting Conference with Leah, her mother and myself. I reiterated the expectations of attendance and completed work. Then, I held my breath and waited.

She came. She worked. She produced. By January she seemed like a "normal" sixth grader. Then she began to take on additional responsibilities. She works as a lunchroom helper daily. She works in the Student Council school store and helps with recycling. She has become opinionated and shares readily as we talk about current events. She asks for help when she doesn't understand something. Classroom friends gave her a birthday party at the Y last Saturday. She is respected and valued. She is engaged and successful. She's going to be fine; she's gained her identity; she is a strong young lady. I am pleased.

∞

Chue was in my classroom for just one year. When I met him, he was a tall, shy seventh grader who didn't smile and hardly spoke. English was his second language and he just wasn't comfortable using it even though he could speak it. He kept his eyes lowered. Chue's academic skills were normal; his reluctance to speak was not. He needed to feel comfortable talking to others — friends and adults.

In order to help Chue I needed to enlist the help of his classmates. I told Chue we needed to share his goal with the class and received his permission. I began the discussion, "Why do you think Chue doesn't talk with you? What might he be feeling?" The students shared a lot of responses. "What do you think we can do to help him?" Again, the students shared suggestions. We agreed we would all help, not to force Chue, but to encourage him.

I don't know how to describe the magic of children helping each other, but I know it works. Slowly Chue's voice was able to be heard by a partner. Gradually he would talk in a small group. In March we agreed that Chue would be our "go-for." He would need to take messages to the office and other teachers. At first this was too frightening, and he took another student along. But, in time, Chue was able to handle this responsibility. The task stretched his ability to speak to other adults and be understood.

Chue is currently a successful 8th grader. Of course, I don't expect him to sign up for the debate team, but he is communicating appropriately with other students and staff. It was a scary process for Chue, but he did it. When I happen to see him in the hall, I hear a clear, "Hi Launa," and I'm proud of this kind young man.

-∞-

Morgan is a very bright sixth grader. He learns incessantly. His broad knowledge of science is richer than most adults'. He spends weekends creating new electronic devices which he demonstrates at school. And, he consistently refuses to do school assignments. When he came into my classroom in January as a fourth grader, he was significantly depressed. He was shut down and morose. He moped through the days. His written assignments never amounted to more than three lines punctuated with glaring spelling errors. I asked him to read a novel for

The secret lies in respecting the pupil.

— *Ralph Waldo Emerson*

a book group. He sat on the edge of the group during discussions, but never read the book. I asked him (as a fourth grader) to come to a math instructional lesson on sixth grade multiplication of fractions. He said it was too easy and tuned out. It was obvious my strategies needed to change drastically if Morgan was going to be engaged.

First I had a whole class discussion about differences. We listed all the ways the students looked differently, acted differently, had different talents and different skills. I asked if I should treat them all exactly alike. Of course, their consensus was NO. Then I started making deals with Morgan. If he wouldn't cooperate with a book group what was he willing to read? "Science, I only read science." So, I encouraged science reading and slowly Morgan began reading at school. But unfortunately, our school library science collection did not keep him stimulated enough. On days without a "good science book" he chose to "read the dictionary" rather than anything else.

As I understood his math skills I marveled at his thinking strategies. With a calculator this fourth grader easily handled ninth grade concepts. However he hadn't memorized his multiplication tables. With clarity he stated, "It's ridiculous to memorize them; adults all use calculators. Why can't I?" Internally I had to agree with Morgan, but externally I explained he wouldn't be allowed to use a calculator on the mandated tests so I'd like him to learn the tables and show how smart he is in math.

Morgan's visual-spatial intelligence surpassed his significantly great logical-mathematical intelligence. As a fourth grader he created a double dodecahedron for his Valentines container. This year as a sixth grader he looked at an one inch design of a "rotatable ring of tetrahedrons", found a large roll of paper and enlarged it fourteen times. The result was a table sized construction which could be rolled, or rotated, or folded into numerous other three dimensional shapes.

Morgan did not complete many of the class assignments. He was unsuccessful doing third grade spelling in the fifth grade. But, when given the California Achievement Tests in reading, writing (students can use dictionaries) and math, Morgan was in the 90th percentile on each test. He hadn't done the "work" but he certainly had the skills. He was learning a lot all the time, but refusing to cooperate with even marginally traditional expectations. His mother and I talked often, fretted often, designed new strategies and consoled one another.

"By respecting students and believing in their ability, value, and self-directing powers, teachers can spend less time in trying to force students to learn, and more energy in developing an exciting and appealing environment for learning to occur."

— Purkey and Novak

As Morgan began sixth grade I admitted to myself that I had nothing to offer this young person but a respectful, supportive environment. The regular school curriculum simply did not appeal to him. When pressured by school assignments, he would say it was a waste of time and slump back into a depression. When allowed to control his time and projects he was an interesting, alive learner. When the educational system left him alone Morgan learned expansively.

I began to search for a mentor. For weeks I called scientists I knew. Finally, a thirty-year old at the science museum agreed to meet Morgan and, tentatively, think about a relationship. Their relationship worked splendidly. The man was fascinated by Morgan's current knowledge, and his ability to synthesize new information. Each weekend they worked together, creating with electronics, taking trips, making neon lights and thoroughly enjoying each other's stimulation. At the year's end Morgan proudly announced his mentor was coming to Achievement Day. Finding Morgan a personal mentor was the best thing I'd been able to do for him.

My job is to educate each child who crosses my path to the best of my ability. Morgan did not want anything to do with school learning. It was boring! By connecting him with his mentor I was able to keep him stimulated and learning with great exuberance. My prayer is that the educational systems somehow find the flexibility to allow him to continue learning rather than squash him by forcing system expectations or school failure on him.

-∞-

Margaret is bright and capable. She usually does more work than is expected. She learns quickly, but somehow is very unsure of herself. She speaks very softly in whole class discussions. She cries easily when a friend disagrees with the way she's playing a game. Tears also well up in the corner of her eyes when other students make suggestions about her writing or give her less than a perfect score on a report.

Her lack of internal security haunts her like a shadow, below the surface about to creep through at any moment, during any activity. Fourth grade is awfully young to have to be perfect. Margaret and I talked about her feelings. I discussed my concerns with her parents and sent

> "Learning is something that children do, not something that is done to them."
> —*Jane Healy*

> "When children know uniqueness is respected, they are more likely to put theirs to use."
> — *Dorothy Briggs*

home *Perfectionism, What's Bad About Being Too Good?* by Miriam Adderholdt-Elliott, suggesting both Margaret and her parents read it. I continue to worry. I try to help her be less critical of herself, but it's going to take some time. I'm thankful that our multi-age classroom will allow me to work with her for a number of years.

-∞-

> "Good schools accept the inconvenience that no two kids are alike. Seven kids may get the answer to a problem wrong, but it may be for seven different reasons. To understand those reasons, you have to know each student well enough to know why in each case. Kids learn in different ways. They are interested in different things. So you can't teach in one way."
> — *Ted Sizer*

Erin is another fourth grader. She doesn't appear to have a worry in her entire body. She is always cheerful and laughs easily. She is continually interested in life. "What's that?" "Why does that work?" Self-evaluation is not part of her consciousness; she floats through life, enjoying the moment. She doesn't remember to look at the assignment board. She doesn't think to ask for help when she is stuck, she just changes activities.

Her academic skills are weak. She doesn't pick up number patterns easily, in part I think because she's so in the moment that she isn't seeing relationships. She must have repeated experiences with manipulatives to learn math concepts.

She reads words just fine, but doesn't naturally translate them into meaning so reading doesn't seem to be valuable. The best reading technique for Erin is to have her act out what she is reading, then she internalizes the words and they become alive. Her needs are so very different than Margaret's needs. I need to help Erin connect information and internalize learning. Margaret needs to loosen up and be, rather than constantly worry about her work, and Erin needs to learn to think about what she is doing and what she needs to do.

-∞-

Patrick chose to stay in fifth grade for a second year. At our school we don't retain children against their will. Research studies conclude it is not helpful, but rather harmful. However, when a child is having a difficult time, we discuss "the opportunity" to have one more year of public education by remaining in the same grade. Another year may provide time for the developmentally different child to catch up, and life may be less stressful. The discussion on this opportunity usually begins in January, so both child and parents have ample time to digest the idea. Patrick is upfront about his decision.

Patrick came into our classroom raucously. When he needed help, he'd shout out my name from wherever he sat, oblivious of what I or others were doing. He was smart enough to get his work done but his actions were random; he rarely finished work. He laughed at others attempts to contribute to discussions and intimidated them by "harmless taps on the shoulder," as he disappeared around the corner.

At the beginning of October we took a trip to the University to see a dance performance. He said he couldn't see from our balcony seats and became obnoxious. I felt trapped. I had responsibility for all of my other children, but he needed to be removed from the theater and yet supervised. In our classroom I could separate him from others if I needed to, but in the theater my options were limited.

When we returned to school I had Patrick call his mother and explain how he had behaved. She confirmed that he has trouble behaving in public places. We discussed other problems he was having in our classroom and agreed on a new behavior plan and continuing communication. I was very careful to repeat that Mom was not responsible for how Patrick behaved at school. Patrick needed to be responsible for himself.

My goals for Patrick were very clear: Wait your turn for help; others are just as important as you are; use your time wisely to complete your assignments; respect other people in all ways. Yet each day presented new struggles.

In December we went to a theater-in-the-round to see Margaret perform in a play. This time, although he admitted he could see just fine, he wanted to move away from the class to a seat in the front row. "It's empty. Why can't I move?" He was loud and disruptive, shouting that he didn't want to come to "this dumb old play anyway." I finally changed my seat to be as far from him as possible and he eventually quieted down.

Back at school I confronted him. He had behaved badly twice on trips. I would not take him out of the school again until I felt assured he would handle himself appropriately. He missed the next three field trips. Other teachers in my school were willing to have him work in their classrooms while I took the class on a trip.

Slowly, very slowly he began to settle down. By April I felt I might be getting somewhere. Most of the time he didn't shout out. Sometimes

"Rousseau believed it was essential for adults to have influence over children, but not by giving orders. He attacked the notion that one teaches responsibility by disciplining for obedience . . . He argued that children should be trained to be self sufficient as early as possible. But this should be 'well-regulated freedom' designed to give the child abundant opportunity to learn from experience and natural consequences. In this manner, the child who has been given responsibility to make his own decisions in childhood would be a responsible, disciplined adult."
— *Bendtro, Brokenleg, Bockern*

when he needed help, he not only walked over to where I was but he actually waited for his turn. He still teased others and joked around, but he was less of the class clown. His relationships with the other students had stabilized. He was making friends.

Another field trip was scheduled. He really wanted to go. We sat together while the rest of the class was reading silently, reviewed my expectations and planned his actions, step by step. I asked, "When you get on the bus, what are my expectations?" "When we enter the museum, how are all students supposed to behave?" Our planning conference lasted fifteen minutes but we had agreed on a detailed plan. Days later he did it. He behaved appropriately and we rejoiced upon returning to school and called his mother with the good news.

Patrick completed his school year a few days later than the rest of the class because his mother and I insisted that he turn in each and every assignment. So Patrick continued to work after the school year finished. But, he did it. He finished all assignments. He was not happy with himself for wasting his school time, but he was also proud that he'd completed the work. I'm pleased I will be working with him again next year. I think a second year of consistent expectations, from both his mother and myself, will give him the habits he needs for success.

There is no single recipe or magical method for helping children grow beyond their problems. The solutions for educating a child are as diverse as there are children. I must walk a fine line between discipline and caring. The individual student must know I care and he must have committed to trusting me before growth will come. I know a caring, trusting community is crucial. As adults, we must keep the end result in mind — educating is not forcing students to walk in the same steps at the same time, it is achieving the final result. It is helping children grow into caring, responsible adults.

"True educational reform will only come about when we make our education appropriate to children's individual growth rates and levels of mental development."
— *David Elkind*

Parent Allies:
The Important Connection

Beginning a relationship ... Goal-setting conferences ... Achievement days ... K-8 by design ... Parents' input ... Committees ... Fundraisers.

Some students are very hard to figure out. They seal themselves behind a tough exterior and will neither reach out for help nor open up when help is offered.

One of my fifth graders had a real chip on her shoulder. Her tone of voice alienated other children. Her view of life was significantly less than half empty, a long way from half full.

It was very obvious that this student's life was not supporting her learning. I needed more guidance, more insightful clues to really understand her problems. I decided to call her mother for strategic advice.

The mother worked long hours. Finally, reaching her at 7:30 AM, I began our conversation gently. "I'm really concerned about your daughter. I'm wondering if you can help me understand how to make school more successful for her. She is alienating others with her tone of voice and her attitude. Can you help me figure out how to help her?"

Her mother was just as worried. Her daughter was acting the same at home. That was helpful to know in itself. But she continued, revealing a series of unsettling events; experiences far too troubling for a fifth grade child to accept with equanimity.

Early in the school year the girl's grandfather had died. He had just returned from an out-of-town trip and fell asleep on the living room couch. Everyone was home, my student, her mother and a two-year old sibling. After a while there was the awful realization. They couldn't rouse grandfather. They called 911 and the rush of emergency treatment descended on the apartment. Then there was the bewilderment of death.

Her mother told me about other disturbing events in the family, about a terrible fight she'd had with her boyfriend. Her daughter had witnessed the whole thing, the yelling, the physical blows. The mother confided, "I know I need counseling. My daughter needs counseling. But how do I pay for it?"

Further in the conversation came the final, most tragic revelation, "My daughter may also be mad because this weekend I commemorated her sister's death." I inquired further. "Well, four years ago her sister, my infant, died of Sudden Infant Death Syndrome." WOW, my brain clicks. Two important deaths since this child was six years old. No wonder she has a heavy shield!

The mother then expressed her concern about her daughter's deteriorating relationship with the family's two year old. We talked and talked. My purpose was to gain insights on why my student was so negative, why she wasn't relating to others in a "normal" way. I found my answers. At this time it was unreasonable to expect this ten-year old to behave the same as others. Her life experiences have taken a different, darker path. She has been dealt a difficult hand, and I must plan the cards with her.

Notice, I did not "dump" this child's school problems on her mother. I probed. I tried to really listen and hear. I am pleased the mother shared as much as she did. I have a much clearer picture of the situation and how I need to approach it. Understanding the child and the home circumstances helps me to better plan for this student's success. Through the parent's eyes I see another side of my troubled student.

-∞-

Parents play a vital role in the effective education of our students. Parents must believe the teachers really want their child to learn. They must trust the teacher. There are many ways I build trust through communication. I involve parents in goal setting. I invite them to our classroom. I give them information on classroom activities.[1] Maslow's hierarchy of basic needs (which are belonging, freedom, power and fun) apply just as much to parents as they do to children.

Communication is an important element in a positive parent-school relationship. My school emphasizes communication from the first week when we invite parents to an orientation evening. After a short introduction to our school in the gymnasium there are two twenty minute sessions in our classrooms. This is the heart of the evening.

As parents arrive I greet them and encourage them to look around our classroom to get a feel of our environment. I begin our session by explaining my commitment to nurturing success for each child. I explain a bit about learning styles and the importance of my understanding each child's strengths. I encourage parents to be my partners as I learn about their children. I explain: "The better I understand your children individually, the better I can plan for their success." I speak of developmental differences and the need for children to construct concepts rather than being told. I explain the need for children to make mistakes, and ask parents to let their children do their own homework, rather than parents hovering over the child to make sure everything is done correctly. I give specifics on how I handle spelling, proofreading, math and reading groups. I answer concerns, and then schedule appointments for Goal Setting Conferences. This orientation begins a valuable relationship of understanding between myself and the parents.

The Goal Setting Conference is the second time I meet parents. These conferences take place as soon as I can schedule them during September and October. These conferences enable parents and students to communicate their hopes, dreams and concerns for the school year. My role is to listen and ask questions. I ask the student, "What are you already good at?" "Have you thought about what is important for you to learn this year?" Students who have been at our school other years often come to the goal setting conference full of ideas. They have learned to be thoughtful about setting goals.

After the student shares his ideas I direct the conversation to the parents. "How do you feel about your child's goals?" Again I listen. Trust is deepened when teachers are truly interested in the parents' and child's opinions. "Does your child have other strengths I should know about?" "Do you have other areas of concern, or other goals you'd like to see accomplished?" Parents are the resident experts on my students. They are intimately knowledgeable about their own child's history and way of approaching the world. I can learn a lot by listening to what is said, and unsaid. Listening attentively acknowledges the importance of the child-parent relationship.

Every parent is emotionally invested in his child; the child is prized. Sometimes teachers see only the mass of thirty students, forgetting the specialness of each individual child for the parents. As a parent I want the very best for my child; as a teacher I must give my students that *best* I deeply want for my own child.

I begin to fill out the Goal Setting form, which is based on Gardner's multi-intelligences (see chapter 6). The first goal category is Intrapersonal Intelligence. This usually consists of goals dealing with responsibility, confidence and self-management. Julie wants to "remember what assignments I have to get done". Morgan's mother wants him to bring school and classroom newsletters home each Wednesday. John has a goal of "figuring out what he likes and dislike". Adrienne wants to get her work done on time and Brian needs to realize how smart he really is.

The second goal area is Interpersonal Intelligence. Students set goals of making new friends, cooperating well in TEAMwork, and solving interpersonal problems immediately rather than letting them fester. Our social skills program is designed to meet many of these goals.

Then I probe for any specific interests, "Do you have something you really want to find out about this year? Some kids want to know more about astronomy or dinosaurs. Others want to learn more about another country. Do you have a specific area you would like to investigate?" These goals are included under World Understanding.

Next our conversation addresses two more traditional areas, Linguistic intelligence ("I want to read two books a month," or "I want to read science fiction this year"), and Logical-mathematical ("I want to remember all my fractions," or "I want to learn negative numbers").

Visual-Spatial goals include geometry, spatial relationships and visual art. One child's goal is "to learn to draw in perspective." Another student claims, "I made a dodecahedron last year. I want to make more complicated shapes this year."

Bodily-kinesthetic goals tend to relate to physical education class, "I want to get the Presidential Physical Fitness Award," and Musical goals to singing, "I'm going to take the choir option this year." But these goals often relate to educational experiences beyond the school day — a basketball team, soccer at the park, or private instrument lessons.

The last entry deliberately deals with "Other goals in your life beyond the classroom" One child assures his mother, "This year I'm going to keep my room clean." Another child wants a dog and promises, "I'll do all of the jobs when we get a dog. I walk him and feed him and train him! I really will!"

I listen and record what both the child and parent want. I may not know the child well enough to assure the parents a goal is reasonable and will be definitely achieved, but I do know what is desired and I will try to help each student reach his goals.

At the end of the conference, all present sign at the bottom, signifying agreement on the plan, and I give the student or parent a copy of the completed form. A few weeks later, I help each child translate each goals into an affirmation. The affirmations are posted in our room and help our focus energy toward achieving the goals.

Each Goal Setting conference takes about a half hour. It is time well spent because it promotes positive communication between teacher, the parents and student. I learn the parents' and the student's expectations. I get a feel of the relationship between parent and child while establishing the groundwork for fluid communication and mutual trust. This relationship is very valuable as I proceed through the school year.

By the end of October I have met with most parents at school twice — once during the group orientation in our classroom, and once privately for their goal setting conference. Yet, some parents are hesitant to come to school; they may not have had a positive experience with schools before. If they don't respond to general invitations, I make a phone call. I share the importance of goal setting and ask if transportation is a problem, or if I may come to their home for a conference. Though home visits take more of my time, I consistently make the visits if I am welcome. My success with a child is always greater when I have established a positive relationship with a parent.

∞

It has been said that information is power. Parents need appropriate and understandable information about their child's progress, and what is happening in the school. This information raises the parent's comfort level and promotes further involvement with our school. Our weekly school newsletter and monthly classroom letter help give parents this important information.

In December and May, we hold Achievement Days. I invite parents to join our class and review their child's portfolio.[2] Portfolios are a collection of the students actual work plus self-evaluation. Some parents

"American public schools are being stripped of their monopoly. Parents are becoming increasingly sophisticated about the differing needs of their children."

— *Edward Fiske*

stop on their way to work early in the morning. Others come at noon with a special lunch to share with their child. I greet them as they arrive and chat as students continue working in a reasonably normal way.

The student and parent find a cozy corner to review the portfolio. Slowly, page by page, the child explains the contents of the portfolio. "Mom, this is the story I wrote the first week of school. My cursive is a lot better now. Look at my latest story."

"Here's my Bones Learning Log. I drew the skeleton of a rabbit on this page. Do you know what's inside bones?" The child savors the undivided attention.

Carefully the parent and child teams review all of the items: reports, records of books read, self-portraits in charcoal, and end-of-week self-evaluations. There are also journals and self-report interest questionnaires. There are numerous learning style assessments and the MMTIC student personality report form. While students explain what they have learned about their learning style preferences I circulate, responding to any questions or concerns. However, the substantial, important conversation is between the child and her parents.

One of the parents, Nancy Gaschott, reviewed her impression of Achievement Day.[3]

"It is December, 1991. I am sitting with my daughter in the hall outside her classroom, looking through a folder of the work she has done since the beginning of the school year. All around us are other children and other parents, eating lunches, looking through folders, and exploring the classroom. This is Achievement Day, the special time set aside for parents to review the first half of the school year. I read with great pleasure my child's booklets and stories, admire the illustrations, read the reports of the computerized standard skills assessments, ask about a project, examine the science experiment. After an hour or so she walks me to the building entrance and I hug her good-bye; I go back to work, she goes back to her classroom.

"Achievement Day, as its name announces, focuses on the positive: we will show what we have achieved. The experience is designed to be full of content and information. It is meant to be a sharing between the student and the parent. It is tactile—I can see and hear and smell and feel the work my daughter has done. It is interactive: her teacher is present; the three of us may discuss some aspect of the work. It is empowering to me: I come away with a better understanding of my child's abilities and needs.

"But it would be a lot simpler to sit back and wait for the traditional biannual report card to show up, because the Achievement Day model of student evaluation demands a lot of parents. Not only must we find a way to get to the school, sometimes leaving work to do so, we must also accept a fundamentally different model of evaluation than the one we experienced as grade school students.

"A report card is definite. It says A or C, B or F. It is authoritative. Mine were stamped with the seal of the school district, and signed by both the teacher and the principal. And report cards offer an impressive long list of subjects, each one paired with a grade, from music to science, arithmetic to physical education.

"Achievement Day, on the other hand, encourages parents to enter into the pedagogy of the Whole Child as Learner. It urges us to abandon the expectations we bring from our own report card days. It offers an opportunity to witness to the fact that children learn differently, have different skills, strengths, paces, abilities. It asks us to encourage our wonderfully unique children to learn the way they learn best. And, ultimately, it challenges us to enter into the educational experience itself."

Seeing the actual materials a student has created gives parents greater information than a letter grade. Parents are charmed, delighted and impressed with their child's record of activity. And, very importantly, the student is full of pride. Even if every parent doesn't make it to Achievement Day, every student still shares with pride because our principal and social worker stop by to "adopt any student who wants to share." These adults enjoy going over the work and making positive comments, just as a child's parent would have done.

Achievement Day isn't the only time parents can join our daily activities. I encourage parents to join us anytime, any day. A few parents volunteer in our room on a weekly basis. Others stop in to chat when they need to confer with their child about a change in after-school arrangements, or need to bring them something, or pick them up for a dental appointment. When parents stop in, I encourage them to stay for a while just to sense the flavor of that particular day. The more a parent understands the child's school life, the greater support I have in reaching our mutual goal, the child's success. I want every parent to feel comfortable stopping by for an impromptu conference if it is needed to further that child's success. If a parent takes the time to call or come by,

I take the time to talk. Sometimes my "curriculum" is delayed with this parent talk time, but I believe it is crucial to communicate if the parent or the child feels frustrated.

Parents' involvement in our K-8 school is fostered on purpose by our design. When a child starts kindergarten the parent knows he will be with us for nine years. Parents get to know the building and the staff because parents know they'll be around for quite a while, usually more years than they can currently imagine their child growing.

This longevity is far different from my feeling about my daughter's two year junior high school. By the time I figured out the right people to talk to at her junior high, the first year was about over. The second year I got little response to my concerns, I think in part, because the staff knew I would be gone the next year. With such a short stay, there was no staff motivation to take my parental concerns very seriously.

A K-8 school has time to build a parental community. It's worth parents' investment of time and energy because this community will be effecting their child for a long time. We purposely choose to be a K-8 school for this reason, and for developmental appropriateness.

Parents are also more involved because of our multi-age classroom arrangement. A student usually stays with a teacher for two or three years. This benefits the students, since the teacher understands their learning style and interests, but it also benefits the parents. Parents invest more in their relationship with the teacher because of the longevity. Parents gain a sense of comfort with the teacher's style and feel more comfortable calling with questions. Teachers seem less remote, more accessible. Over time parents and I work together building a relationship of trust and respect so we are able to solve a problem before it blocks their child's learning.

During the May Achievement Day I receive parting hugs, not just from students, but from the parents whom I've know for a long time. Often students visit years later, or a proud parent stops by to share bits of pleasure about their child who has blossomed in high school. In many ways our multi-age K-8 school in the middle of urban Minneapolis feels like a one-room schoolhouse community. Our chosen structure fosters a caring partnership of parents and staff united for the education of children.

Our school welcomes parental insight and input in choosing the

Speaking to parents, "Your own attitudes toward learning and the time that you spend with your child in learning activities may have a greater impact on his academic success than all of his teachers combined."

— *Thomas Armstrong*

child's next teacher. Each spring parents are sent a "Teacher Preference" form. Parents and students are encouraged to visit other classrooms to sense where the student would learn best. Different teacher styles work well for different children and usually a parent can sense a good match. Each year 80+% of our parents turn in the preference form. When we begin organizing classes for the following year we start with the parent's preference, then adjust to balance race, gender, teacher recommendations and special needs. Parents don't always get their first choice but we try.

-∞-

Parents play other important roles in our school both with students and on committees. We encourage participation in the classrooms. Some parents are comfortable working side by side with teachers; some parents are comfortable handling a book group or reading to children. Other parents come to share a particular skill or hobby. Some parents teach an eight-week "Options" mini-course to a multi-age group of interested students from many classrooms. Other parents help by preparing materials, or work at home on projects such as word processing children's stories.

All of our school's regular committees include parents. Our site-based council deals with school finances and major policy decisions. Parents and staff on the "Process Task Force" reflect on the mood of the school throughout the year and plan staff development topics. A parent-staff task force interviews perspective staff members, including our principal. The Arts Task Force plans enriching art events, interviews prospective artists-in-residence, and brings special art experiences into our school. Another group deals with our building and playground (a constant source of frustration since we are housed in an old, inadequate building on half a city block). Some task forces are created for short term projects; many are a year's commitment. Parents are constantly invited to use their expertise and interests to support the activities of our school.

-∞-

Parents are also prime participants in our fundraising activities. However rather than focusing simply on raising money we also focus on the fun in fundraising. We have chosen fundraisers which promote a sense of community spirit. Our spring bedding plant sale is a great time to connect with other parents and chat. The winter used book sale, sponsored by the student council, brings parents and children together for a good cause. In the fall, a local Renaissance festival involves volunteer families in the fun of costume and role-playing. Every few years parent and staff quilters create a special quilt which is raffled off. These "fun" fundraisers are very different than raising money by sending students door to door to sell. Our fundraisers raise our community spirit as well as money.

I am successful teaching children, in part, because parents are working together with me as a team. Together we strive to have each child develop toward full potential. Building a trusting and relaxed communication between home and the classroom, enlisting parents as allies is a very important process for my success as a teacher.

-∞-

[1] *A Parent's Guide to Innovative Education*, by Anne Wescott Dodd (The Noble Press: 1992), is an excellent resource for parents.

[2]. For more information on portfolios read *Multiple Intelligence: The Theory in Practice* by Howard Gardner (Harper Collins: 1993).

[3] Nancy Gaschott, "Achievement Day," *Consortium for Whole Brain Learning*, Vol. 7, Number 3. 3348-47th Ave. So., Mpls. MN 55406.

Language: Building Blocks for Thought

Drawing and writing ... Journals ... Learning logs ... Story writing ... Imagery ... Pre-writing and re-writing ... Essays ... Quality reports ... Reading must connect ... Book groups ... Before reading ... Vocabulary ... Carbo's audio method ... Mistakes ... Use it don't lose it ... SQUIRT.

Writing and reading are inextricably tied to experiences, to drawing, speaking and thinking. Language is dependent on experience. Without experiences a child has no internal understanding of words. Words are symbolic shortcuts, substitutes for experience. Children begin learning by experiencing their world nonverbally, without understanding the meaning of sounds. Later they begin to understand that sounds relate to objects and their brains develop the neural pathways which support listening and speaking. Finally reading and writing are developed as representations of experiences and thoughts.[1] Language gives our species the potential of complex abstract thought.

This chapter begins with the drawing/writing connection and continues to reading strategies. When children internalize the cycle of their thoughts being drawn or written and read, they can be convinced of the importance of reading and writing.

∞

Young children need to draw. Drawings are a visual representation which ease children into the power of written symbols. Drawing is an important step in developing the internal symbolic understanding needed for successful use of language. Student drawings are labelled with words, thus gently transferring the child's meaning to the shapes of letters. In the classroom it is important to maintain this connection between drawing and writing as visual representations of a child's larger experience.

In order to write, a child must first have something to say. She must believe the abstract letters used by adults carry meaning. Then, and only then, will the child be ready to enter the world of written communication.

Writing is the vehicle of communication. In my classroom writing and drawing begin the first day of school with journaling.[2] I explain, "Journals are for you. I expect you to write and draw in your journal, but what you write and draw is up to you. You may want to write about what you are going to do, or what you have done. You may want to draw a picture of your new bike or pet. You may make a maze or an imaginary creature. You could write a story, a rap or a poem. It's up to you. My expectation is that you use your journal time wisely. I will look through your journal to understand your ideas but I won't correct your journal in any way. Your journal is a record on paper of your ideas. This time is for you. I expect you to be quiet during journal time; afterwards you may share your ideas with your friends, if you'd like."

Some children jump into journaling with a passion. They have ideas to express and they have internalized the purpose of writing and drawing. Other children sit with the white blank paper staring up at them. They have no idea what to do. They either have not internalized the cycle of representing thoughts with symbols or, maybe, adults have devalued their thoughts. Regardless, the cycle of experiences, thoughts and symbolic representation is not completely developed. To help these students I read a *daily idea* from *Writing Down the Days*[3] before they begin to write in their journals.

I play background calm music to fill the silence during the journal writing period.[4] It's time for my students to go inside their heads without distraction. It's time to take thoughts and give them life in words and drawings.

I move around the room to befriend children who are stuck. "Julie, are you stuck today? Would you like me to get you some markers so you can draw a picture?" "Devin, didn't you play soccer yesterday? How about writing a story about your game?" Children who do not comfortably draw and write for the sake of self-expression are not going to be successful learning technical aspects of writing. Unfortunately, when children have not internalized the language cycle in the developmentally appropriate years from four to seven, it takes a long time to repair this important building block.

"Learning Logs" like journals, include both writing and drawing, but they serve a different purpose. A Learning Log is a record of thoughts and ideas during a specific investigation. I use Learning Logs to record math projects, science investigations and social studies. Last spring my classroom studied plants and created "Plant Learning Logs". The first page was a pretest, a gauge of what students already knew. I asked students to "name as many plants as you can in two minutes. Explain why most plants are green. Write down how plants reproduce themselves. List ten ways we use plants. Have you (not your parent) grown any plants? Please explain."

The body of this Learning Log contained records of planting seeds, watering and watching; rooting sweet potato tubers; studying different leaves and drawing the vein organization; learning about the "sex life" of plants and drawing the flower parts; and predictions on numerous plant experiments I brought into the room. At the end of this unit of study, students reflect on this new knowledge and convey their feelings about our plant study in the Logs. Then they make a fancy cover, create a title for their Learning Log books, number the pages, and make a table of contents. Students proudly share their final results and we compare our Learning Logs with published books about plants.

Learning Logs may be created on any topic of study. They are a natural way to record, and reflect on, information. They also help children internally connect the writing and drawings in published books with their own life experiences.

∞

We also practice creative story writing. Again, the first condition of success is having something to say. A child can't write if he has nothing to write about. For this reason I never assign a narrow writing topic but rather focus students' energies in one of two ways: by suggesting that they demonstrate a skill, for example a "Conversation Story" or through an imagery experience which elicits sensory information for the student.

A skill focus story reinforces any of many specific skills. We often start with a good model of the skill, for instance, reading a great character description in a favorite book. Or we may discuss the important elements of portraying a character and form groups to create some very vivid

"If we taught our children to speak in the way that we teach them to write everyone would stutter."
— *Mark Twain*

descriptions. Then I assign a story which includes "great descriptions of your characters". These activities build a store of creative fuel before beginning to write.

At another time I may have gone over the techniques of writing conversation and dialogue, pointing out the commas and quotation marks which enclose the words which come from someone's mouth. Or we may have brainstormed ways to write the word "said" without using "said". One year student groups listed over a hundred different ways to say "said". The challenge was great fun and stories after the exercise were alive with expressive conversations.

A second method of stimulating quality writing is to have students imagine their characters and action with significant sensory detail before they begin to write. I prepare by having my students get paper and pencil out for use at the end of this imagination adventure. Then I ask them to get physically relaxed and comfortable. "Now, close your eyes so you can concentrate on what happens in your imagination rather than the things in our classroom. Letting your imagination 'go' is difficult for some people. Some people see a hazy picture; other see in technicolor. Some people hear or smell in their imagination better than seeing pictures. Don't force ideas in your imagination. If you aren't comfortable with your eyes closed (some children aren't) focus on one uninteresting spot on the ceiling, for visual thinker, or down at your toe, if you're kinesthetic, and project your imagination there. While you are waiting for others to become settled, see your own name in your imagination . . . notice the colors of each letter . . . change the sizes of the letters and enjoy your own name . . . ."

I use imagery to enrich student essays about particular units of study. When I wish to enhance our study of animal habitats, I incorporate a session of vivid imagining. Waiting until my students are quiet, I begin slowly, giving ample time for them to use their imaginations.

"In your imagination see a friendly dog. Notice its size . . . Notice the texture of its fur . . . and its colors . . . Watch it wag its tail as you pet it . . . Now, in your imagination, while the back remains a dog, change the front part of your dog into a cat. See this new animal running and playing . . . Notice how the fur of the front and back join together, whether it's a sharp clear line or subtle changes . . . Now, change the back into a zebra . . . Enjoy this special creature. Give it a name. You can create

"I close my eyes when I want to see."

—*Paul Gamarin*

other new animals so now change the front into an elephant . . . . Now shrink it smaller and smaller, so small it is almost lost in the grass. Change the back into a snake all striped and strong. See the whole animal from front trunk to back tip. Now look at the environment around this ele-snake. Notice where it's living. Notice the plants, the ground, the sunshine or the shadows. Now, change the front into a bird with broad wings to balance the snake tail. See it circle in the air and land smoothly . . . Change the back into a monkey, and the front . . . into a dolphin. Change the back again to whatever pops into your imagination. Change the back again. Continue to change parts until you create an animal you really like. It may be something completely new, or you may return to one of the animals you have already created . . . . Spend a moment understanding how your special animal is put together. See the colors clearly. Notice the textures. You may want to pet it to get a feel of the textures . . . . Get close enough to notice if your new creature has a distinctly pleasant smell, or maybe an unpleasant smell. Give your creature a name . . . . Now, notice its surroundings. It may live in a forest, or a meadow, or a desert, or underwater. See its environment clearly . . . . Notice the small things in the environment. Be aware of the temperature, the variations of color and the smells. Watch it as it gets some food. Notice how it manages to eat. Finally, see if there are other animals like it around. Maybe it lives in a group, or maybe it lives alone. Understand how your special creation interacts with its environment. When you understand the details of your animal's life — its food and eating habits, its relationship with other animals and its habitat, then bring your attention back to our classroom, quietly open your eyes and begin to make notes and pictures about your animal."

There is a rustle of movement as students pick up the pencils and paper, but I've trained them to stay with their own thoughts.

Most students are full of ideas after they use their imaginations. But, since imagining isn't easy for everyone I move quietly through the students to support anyone who is not fluidly writing or drawing. I pose questions to encourage further thinking. I encourage students to make decisions about their animals and to fill a page with specific details. This is the pre-writing stage, the gathering of ideas to formulate later. If students do not successfully complete this stage they have little to work with when writing.

"When I examined myself and my methods of thought, I came to the conclusion that the gift of fantasy has meant more to me than my talent for absorbing positive knowledge."

—Albert Einstein

A first draft of the creative story is due about three days after the pre-writing experience. Then students share their stories with three or four other students to get feedback and suggestions. A final draft is due within the following four days. Students need significant time to write; ideas don't solidify in just one class period. The incubation process of getting an idea, writing, reflecting and rewriting helps thoughts to be clarified and developed. Quality writing is not a one time expression to be left and forgotten.

Other writing tasks, whether poetry or letter writing, require the same steps to insure the success of all students. A writing concept is taught or reviewed (not necessarily on the same day however), stimulation is provided for the students to generate ideas, adequate incubation time is provided between the initial stimulation and the due date, and there is feedback from peers who have been coached to be helpful.

∞

Essay writing requires the same extensive pre-thinking in order to generate ideas, but it necessitates different organization strategies. Webbing, also known as clustering, is a very useful writing aid, enabling students to more fully explore an essay's content.[5] Once again it is important to continue to brainstorm the web until a page is full. The more ideas a student has initially the richer her writing is likely to be.

After students have filled a page with randomly articulated ideas, I begin directions, "Now, look at the ideas on your page. Look to see if any ideas fit together. If you find some that do, draw arrows between them. Then decide which idea you want to start with, and label it #1. Continue writing numbers to sequence your ideas. You don't need to use all of the ideas in your web, so if you think something doesn't really fit you can cross the idea out. Once you have planned an order for your ideas, write an introductory paragraph so your reader will understand your plan." Essays become easy when students have learned this organization process.

Report writing is an elaboration of essay writing. I begin teaching how to make 3x5 note cards. Some students prefer to use a small pad of paper instead of keeping track of individual note cards. I model source cards on the chalkboard with title, author, company, and date are placed

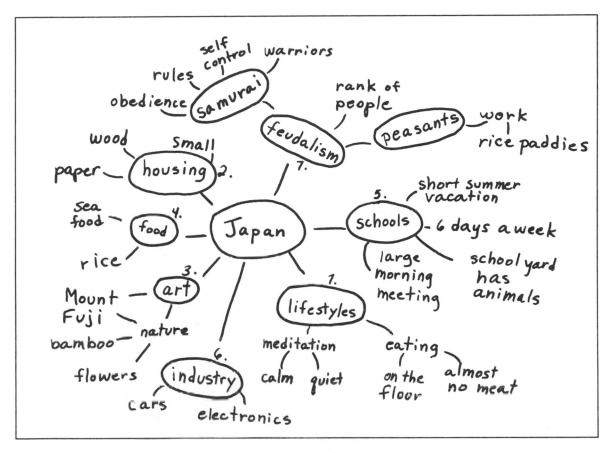

in the center, with the source number in the upper left corner. Note cards use the source number in the same upper left corner and the page number in the upper right. Each note card records a single idea. Writing just one idea can be difficult for some students because it takes analysis and evaluation. I model writing a single fact on the chalkboard and check on students' note taking as they begin, helping them learn to rephrase information.

Notecards allow students to gather information without having to determine the sequence or importance of the information. It delays ordering and organizing until there is a wealth of information, much like the webbing technique. When students learn the process of note taking they gain the ability to organize information.

As my students learn note taking correctly they have an important skill for future independent work. When students feel they have enough information I teach them to sort similar cards into piles (like our arrows on a web) and then number the piles (like ordering essay ideas). Then I show children how to take each pile and arrange the cards in a reasonable order. Finally I teach how to write a topic sentence. "Put a colored card on top of each pile for the topic sentence. A topic sentence tells what the topic is about without giving too much information. For example, 'I will explain about Martin Luther King's childhood.'"

It took years for me to learn to directly teach each step of the report writing process. Now I send these direction sheets home as students begin to write a report so parents and students can review the plan.

Creating a Quality Report

1. Choose a topic you really are interested in.
2. Find three or more sources. Make source cards.
3. Take notes on 3X5 cards, or a small tablet. Write only one concept on a card and use your own words. (This requires evaluation of ideas and rephrasing the idea rather than copying.)
4. When you have 50 or more cards and feel sure you have covered the topic, sort into piles of similar content.
5. Sort each pile to put the cards in the order you want to use them.
6. Write a topic sentence for each pile on a different colored card. Put it on top and bind with a rubber band.
7. Put all of the piles into the order you want to use them. Number the piles.
8. Write an introductory paragraph for the whole report. The first sentence should state the topic, but not give information. The following sentences tell what will be covered in the report, in the order it will be covered.
9. Decide what pictures, maps, etc. you want to include in your report and create them or have them copied. If you photocopy be sure to cite your source.
10. Now begin writing. Put your introductory paragraph on one page. Start a new page for each pile. Make the topic sentence the first paragraph at the top of the page. Double check to be sure all information in this section relates to the topic. Remember all normal writing rules like margins, punctuation, and proofreading for spelling. Put your illustrations in as you write so they fit appropriately with the words describing them.

11. Write a conclusion or summary. Restate what you learned and how you feel about it.

12. Put your source cards in alphabetical order to make a bibliography: Author (last name first), Title (underlined), date of publication, publisher and city. The bibliography is the last page of your report.

13. Number the pages of your report, then create a table of contents with the titles on the left and the numbers on the right.

14. Make an interesting cover that is relevant to your report information. Include the title of the report, your name, color and a visual.

15. After the report is done, create a "Make or Do" project — to share your information with your classmates. This could be a model, a display, a play, or anything that isn't paper and pencil.

16. Your report and "Make or Do" presentation will be evaluated by other students, and I will evaluate them as well.

As reports are turned in I encourage students to look at each others' work. Each student evaluates three reports using a form which rates (0-5 points) the cover, table of contents, introductory paragraph, topic sentences, spelling, punctuation, illustrations, conclusion, bibliography and overall neatness (50 points total). This evaluation process allows students to glean ideas from their peers and it feels good to have many people read and appreciate the significant effort put into the report and project. I evaluate the reports after the peer process and present Excellence Awards to students scoring over 45 points.

-∞-

The teaching of reading has been hotly debated for years because reading, gaining meaning from letters in different arrangements, is at the foundation of our modern society. According to some estimates, a Sunday New York Times contains more print than our Revolutionary War ancestors saw in their entire lifetime.

There is a well kept secret about reading instruction which has been sealed in a silent accord with basal reading companies. I taught many years before I uncovered this secret. The secret is simply that no reading series has ever had a research base to document that it teaches children to read. "Buy our series," the companies say. "It has the best stories." "Buy our series," another declares. "We have an excellent teacher's guide." But they don't promise their system teaches children to read.

As a new teacher I was given a reading series, "Here, use this series to teach students to read." I was naive. I believed the series must teach children to read because powerful people told me to use it. But, my students misbehaved. I must be teaching it wrong, I rationalized and scurried back to the teacher's manual for greater wisdom. It never occurred to me that the reading series simply didn't work.

Reports bemoan students' dismal reading scores. Districts have switched from phonetic series to whole word series and back again hoping, without understanding, that the next series will do a better job.

The truth is a basal reading series won't work for all children because reading is the process of gaining meaning from abstract symbols. Children must be able to relate these abstractions to real experience in order to gain meaning and our students have not had the same experiences. The differences between children's life experiences are greater today than at any time in our public schools' history. Without experiences which relate to the abstract symbols our students will not remember words. Reading about farm animals, for some children, may be familiar. But city kids probably have no experience with farm animals. Without experience children will not ascertain the meaning behind the words. I had the same difficulty with meaning when I tried to read quantum physics. I didn't have the background to link quantum physics to relevant information and thus I didn't remember the content or words.

Human brains sort incoming information to link new information to the old. Our brains pay particular attention to emotional, unusual or interesting information. As we read, information which doesn't connect or have significant interest is thrown out. It is forgotten. These basic brain rules are in effect as any child learns to read.

I teach reading in small groups using real books. Most of the time I select 7-8 books on different topics and grade levels which relate to a larger concept such as our school's last theme, "Changes, Choices, Challenges". For this theme I used Norma Klein's *Confessions of an Only Child* (reading level 2.4, a poignant story of an only child whose mother is pregnant), Conrad Richter's *The Light in the Forest* (reading level junior high, about a boy raised by the Lenni Lenape Indians then

"If we wish to induce children to become literate persons, our teaching methods should be in accordance with the richness of the child's spoken vocabulary, his intelligence, his natural curiosity, his eagerness to learn new things, his wish to develop his mind and his comprehension of the world, and his avid desire for the stimulation of his imagination — in short, by making reading an activity of intrinsic interest."
—*Bruno Bettelheim & Karen Zelan*

returned to his proper white family), Elizabeth Yates' *Amos Fortune Free Man* (reading level fifth, a story of a black slave obtaining his freedom and helping others), a book about dinosaurs (I always offer a nonfiction choice because some students do not like "stories"), and four other books.

I have rarely paid regular price for these sets of paperback books — I can't afford them on my school budget. But I have enlisted parents to watch for good books at garage sales and library sales. Over the years I've managed to collect a closet full of multi-copy books. Sometimes I only have two copies of a book, but those work well for reading pairs, an alternative to a larger group. I also rely on my colleagues to have sets of some books as we help each other bring the best to our students.

When I set the books out on the table for students to look over and choose which books they'd prefer to read, there is a flurry of activity. It's not a first-come situation so speed isn't important, it's simply that my students are excited. "I read that one, it's really good!" "Mom got this one for me." "I want to be in this group." There's good conversation about the books, the authors and related literature.

Students sign their preferences on the book chart and I strive to balance the groups. I prefer groups no larger than eight students in order to include everyone in the discussions. Sometimes a group is only three students, a nice size for children who are having some difficulty reading.

Each new book group is distinctly different. Some groups need a lot of my time to help them discern relevant ideas and engage in quality discussions. Other groups want to read the book quickly, thoroughly concentrating on the plot in an intense, short period. Some groups have capable student leaders who can facilitate in-depth discussions without me. I check in with these students but don't "teach" them. They learn for themselves.

When a book group meets for the first time I ask questions to focus my students' attention. "Have you ever felt confused (or frustrated, or scared — whatever the key emotion portrayed by the story)?" I listen. Too many teachers speed through this stage; I relish it. The more my students' connect with their own similar experiences, (4MAT, Quadrant 1) the more they will relate to the story, learn new vocabulary, understand the characters, and enjoy the plot.

As the spontaneous sharing slows, I ask the students to skim the next few pages as I model using a blank card, sweeping the lines fast enough

"Psychologists, psycholinguists, and reading theorists have long maintained that the background information a reader has on any particular topic has a powerful influence on how well the reader will comprehend that topic."
—*Richard Sinatra*

so reading is impossible. Then we close the book. "What words did you pick up?" The students recall a word, then more. "What pictures or headings do you remember?" Sharing continues. "What do you think this story may be about?" Predictions are important; they alert the brain to evaluate as the story is being read.

I choose a limited number of words to discuss before we read. Many words are new only in the sense that children haven't read them before. They have often heard the words but just haven't seen them in print. When I introduce specific vocabulary, I ask the children to go to the actual page, skim for the word and then discuss it in context. I write the word on the board so everyone can see it and we study its configuration (shape is a visual clue) and phonics (a sequential, auditory clue). Global learners need to see the word in context to make sense out of it. One study concluded 17 out of every 19 poor readers are global learners.[6] Because global learners are more at risk, I introduce new vocabulary first in the context of the story. Then I write the word alone and help students analyze it. I do not label my students global or analytic, but I know I have both and I teach new words in both processing styles.

Vocabulary development is valued in most reading programs. Yet the suggested teaching methods are sadly simplistic; the teacher introduces the words and the students are to remember them. The brain's memory functions much like a card catalogue. If an entry is listed by title, author, and subject, there are three ways of accessing it. If it is only cataloged by the title it is more difficult because there is only one chance to find it.[7] When a vocabulary word has been stimulated through all of the perceptual modalities, visual, auditory and tactile/kinesthetically, as well as linked to previous experiences or emotions, it has many more ways to be retrieved from memory.

Traditionally students were given a list of words and another of definitions to match. Then they were tested. Today there are many more engaging ways to learn vocabulary. The teaching methods in the "Word-A-Day" program[8] can easily be translated to story vocabulary. Students can draw pictures of the word, create 3-D displays, act out the word, or bring in objects related to the word. Words and definitions can be made into puzzle piece task cards, flip chutes or electroboards .[9] Words can be learned by creative writing or by integrating new words into everyday life. Students can be in charge of identifying the new words in a story, writing them on cards and teaching them to the rest of the group. Instead of word cards flashed to the whole group, each child can have a card to explain to the group. After once around the circle, students pass the cards to the right three times and then go around again with each student explaining his new word. Brains pay attention to the unusual. There are a thousand variations to teach vocabulary so I don't stick to a routine method because it bores the brain. I engage all perceptual modalities and relate words to students' personal experiences.

How do adults continue to learn new vocabulary? It certainly isn't with formal methods, rather it's by sensing the word in context and, once in a while, checking a dictionary. Children often learn vocabulary in the same way and are slowed down by teachers "teaching".

Now the story has been introduced and my students are ready to read. To promote the greatest success and enjoyment for each reader I provide a variety of reading environments. Some readers prefer to read silently, alone. Other children prefer to read aloud in pairs. Some readers prefer reading in a chair while others sprawl across the pillows in the corner. Some readers do better with a blank card shielding future lines from their visual screen; others need to subvocalize. Some readers do better using a transparent color overlay;[10] other readers prefer dim light.

∞

I've completed three pre-reading steps: I've connected the story to my children's lives with an anticipatory discussion. I've developed vocabulary for both global and analytical learners, and I've provided for differences in physical comfort while reading.[11] Now my students read.

Teaching reading in the past often focused on the student's deficits — the skills a child wasn't very good at, in hopes of improving their skills. Marie Carbo has helped change the focus from one on deficits to one that utilizes the student's strengths as the basis for growth. Carbo's recorded book method enables students to simultaneously see and hear the word, facilitating concentration on the meaning of the words.[12]

Carbo's audio book tapes are pre-recorded by the teacher in short sections. The student identifies with the teacher's voice and the teacher knows the student well enough to appropriately and deliberately pace the words, the phrasing and the expression. The student is able to listen to

"Woodrow (Wilson) did not learn his letters until he was nine or learn to read until he was eleven. There are letters from relatives who thought it odd that young Woodrow was so dull ... and expressed sorrow for the parents."
—*Lloyd Thompson*

the audio tape privately, as many times as needed, until he can read the selection fluidly. Then he reads it aloud with pride to the teacher. This recorded book method has research studies attesting to its effectiveness for struggling readers. I have had successes using it and encourage others to try this way of strengthening sluggish readers.

I use a similar method without recording a tape for personal paired reading. The method is easy to teach to adults volunteering in our classroom. I read a short paragraph aloud twice, asking the student to read with me in her head. We talk about the paragraph, then I ask the student to read the same paragraph aloud. If the child falters at all, I don't comment, I simply reread the section so it's modelled once more. This method is effective because the learner sees and hears the words in context.

I never ask students to read aloud without first giving them a chance to read the material first. Many adults do not feel comfortable reading aloud to a group of their peers without practice. I give my students the same respect and the opportunity to prepare. Understanding the meaning and punctuation is a prerequisite to reading aloud with appropriate expression. If a student "mis-reads" a word I gently probe for meaning. I do not immediately correct the "mistake." I ask, "What does that mean to you?" More often than not the student either catches her own mistake or has subconsciously altered the word for improved personal meaning.

A study of first-graders' mistakes revealed that 86% of the mistakes were actually substitutions "that made equal or better sense than the original text."[13] For instance, "Spot can hear me," instead of "Spot can help me." These mistakes are very reasonable for global readers who are seeking meaning from the abstract symbols called words. Omitting words were 6% of the errors and all other errors only 1.4% of the mistakes.[14] My task is to help students glean meaning from the symbols and help students feel reading is a profitable experience for them. Jumping on student mistakes fosters neither of my goals, so I patiently probe for reasons and redirect my strategies.

Once the material has been read I want students to make the content their own. Discussion is just one way to accomplish this. Alternate methods are as abundant as your imagination. One way is to relax your students and ask them to close their eyes to the outer world to "see and hear" the scene in their imagination. Then I carefully reread descriptive portions, with poignant pauses and directions, "Notice the colors in this scene, notice the textures, the smells, the sounds . . . . " Thus, instead of just reading the words, students experience the words.[15]

Other ways to internalize a book are: scripting an original play to act out the characters' essence and actions; or presenting a mock author interview. Students can use a long roll of paper to create a sequential comic strip or create a circular series of pictures with a pie-shaped view window. Children may also create 3-D tagboard story pyramids, or construct pop-up books which picture the story.

As my students' book groups finish reading, they plan a presentation of the book for the whole class. They don't just leave the story but rather translate it into another form of communication by using different art forms. This process requires analysis, evaluation and synthesis. My students do more thinking, using higher thinking processes but cover less content. Reading story after story is not learning; making meaning, linking learnings to previous knowledge and exercising important thinking skills is learning from reading.

∞

Another component of my reading program is SQUIRT. The acronym stands for Super Quiet UnInterrupted Reading Time. This is a daily occurrence.

If children do not adopt the habit of reading for themselves, all of the effort of teaching children to read is wasted. Children don't automatically become "readers" just because they have the skills, they need to learn to value reading for the knowledge and enjoyment it provides. Time spent in SQUIRT achieves this goal. For a half hour each day I expect my students to read books of their own choice. The child chooses what he reads, but not whether he reads.

Children do not automatically know which books will appeal to them. It takes learning and practice. I watch to see who settles down comfortably with a book. Some eyes are focused, the student blissfully unaware of the rest of the classroom. Others are not quite focused and some have not even settled on a choice. First I help children at our book corner, to find something of interest. "What do you like to read?"

When they do not know, I select a couple of books and offer them,

"Pupils in the middle grades still benefit from silent reading time during their regular reading class period, a Univ. of MN study confirms. Students who had spent the most time reading to themselves in reading class had registered the greatest gains. This included both assigned and 'for pleasure' reading."
— *Growing Child Research Review*
December, 1990

"Do you know how to tell if its a good book for you?"

"I don't know."

"Try reading the back cover, then paging through the book a little to look at the pictures or chapter titles. Then stop on any page in the middle of the book and try reading a few paragraphs to feel if you like it."

As the student tries, I look for other possible choices. Book selection skills are often presumed as a kind of "tacit knowledge", knowledge which children are expected to have but have not been taught.

When these children have found something tempting, I check on those students who had chosen books but remain unfocused. Some have settled in but Jason is still unfocused. I approach him with a smile and ask if he likes his book.

Jason responds, "It's not very interesting."

"Why don't you choose another one. Just because you started a book doesn't mean you have to finish it." As he heads for the bookshelf I find his SQUIRT card, the record of his reading. "Jason, on a scale of 1-10 what was your opinion of that last book?"

"It was a three."

"Why?"

"The story was boring."

"Why did you feel that?"

"Nothing happened, all they did was talk about what it was like."

"How about putting that on your evaluation before you find another book."

Jason has reached a level of sophistication about the quality of literature but he was only able to vaguely identify what was wrong. Children learn about quality literature by experiencing books. Jason has just begun.

Reading and writing are necessary skills. Language enables us to create mental representations which soar beyond the real world. I must do whatever it takes to have all of my students become fluent readers and writers. There is no recipe which will help each child learn. Rather I watch and listen to the child, taking clues from the way he is behaving in order to teach his way. It is my responsibility as the professional to help each child to feel as comfortable and successful using language as walking. To do this I must use my own best judgement and basic brain precepts.

∞

[1] For a scholarly discussion of these relationships see Richard Sinatra, *Visual Literacy Connections to Thinking, Reading and Writing* (Charles Thomas: 1986).

[2] *The Creative Journal for Children* by Lucia Capacchione (Shambhala: 1989) is a good resource for further ideas about journaling.

[3] *Writing Down the Days*, by Lorraine Dahlstrom (Free Spirit Publishing: 1991).

[4] Two good sources of music tapes for classroom use are: the Barzak Institute, 800-672-1717, and the Lind Institute, 800-462-3766.

[5] Gabriele Lusser Rico's *Writing the Natural Way* (Tarcher: 1983) is a good resource for further understanding of webbing.

[6] Carbo, Dunn and Dunn, *Teaching Students to Read Through Their Individualized Learning Styles* (Prentice Hall, 1986), p. 20. This is an excellent resource dealing with global/analytic issues and perceptual modalities.

[7] Bob Sylwester, Univ. of Oregon, Eugene, originally used this analogy.

[8] Materials developed by teacher Marlene Glaus. For information send SASE to Box 242, 4575 West 80th Street Circle, Bloomington, MN 55437

[9] Carbo, Dunn and Dunn, Chapter 7.

[10] *60 Minutes*, CBS News, August 20. 1989, Morley Safer, "Reading By the Colors."

[11] Carbo, Dunn and Dunn.

[12] *Ibid.*, p. 117.

[13] Bruno Bettelheim and Karen Zelan, *On Learning to Read: The Child's Fascination with Meaning* (Alfred Knopf: 1961), p. 132. I recommend reading this book for a more complete understanding of children's reading mistakes and implications. It's filled with important insights.

[14] *Ibid.*, p. 132.

[15] A good resource for understanding the importance of imaging in reading is Laura Rose's *Picture This: Teaching Reading Through Visualization* (Zephyr Press: 1989).

Mathematics: A Way of Processing Information

10

The scope ... Pre-testing ... Crucial manipulatives ... Mistakes are clues ... Matt's experience ...
Multiplication and division ... Fractions ... Decimals ... Activities ... Fascinating experiences.

Math is a symbolic language. It is a way of thinking about the world. Like drawing, writing and reading, mathematics needs to be rooted in experience before children can internalize its concepts.

Children in my classroom often are "doing math" without knowing it because math is much more than computation. Math is present in graphing color preferences for this year's school sweat shirt. Math is present in time lines, and longitude/latitude coordinate. Math is planning and organizing a class pizza party. Math is creating an original 3-D Valentines' container.

The precepts for children learning math are the same as for learning everything else — start with what the child already knows and connect new concepts to that base. Students must "construct" an understanding of the number system. They must be able to visualize the "taking out in groups" process of division. Manipulatives must abound at every grade level, because the right hemisphere needs to experience math concepts concretely to learn.

Problem solving is the essence of using math and must be included at every age, every day. Language is the framework around math; it must be an integral part of children's math experience. Students need to read "story problems" and, more importantly, make up their own problems to share with each other.

Six years ago my school began using a computerized instructional management system to pre- and post-test math objectives. Before I had this system I used post-tests from commercial materials to "pre-test" students' skills and understanding. Pre-testing allows me to teach new concepts only to students who 1) don't already know it (because I want all students' work to be "hard enough but not too hard"), and 2) have all the necessary background to be able to learn it. This may sound obvious, or it may sound revolutionary. But in the past teachers simply proceeded with the textbook plan without considering these two important factors of success.

When I get the pre-test results I share the information with my students. Whatever I know about a student's work is shared with the student. There are no hidden secrets. "This is what the pre-test shows you know. This is what you've mastered. This is what you need to learn." Then I invite students to come to a teaching meeting. "I'll be teaching subtracting fractions with common denominators right after this meeting. If you need to learn that, please come." I explain what I am going to teach and I invite students to come. It's easiest for me if all students who need to learn this actually come, but that's not always the case. Some students may be out of the room working on a student council project. Others may be immersed in their creative writing and just can't pull themselves away at the time I begin the lesson. Some children don't learn well from whole group presentations. They will ask a friend to teach them after the friend learns. I've made it clear to my students what they know and what I expect them to learn. I expect my students to be responsible. Being responsible means making choices, and one of the choices is how to learn the material they are held responsible for.

-∞-

When I began my career twenty-some years ago, teachers didn't use manipulatives. Somehow the children were supposed to know what numbers meant. Typically students working without manipulatives had no idea what they were doing, or why. No wonder so many students didn't like math. It was years before educators began to understand children's need to "construct" concepts and thus build their own insights.

Today there is a wide and rich collection of effective manipulatives on the market.[1] We have come to understand that brains need stuff, real stuff to foster an understanding of abstract number concepts, including algebra.[2]

Student mistakes give clear indication of their abstract understandings. Matt was a new fifth grader in my class. I gave Matt an overview test to get a sense of his math skills. He missed a simple subtraction problem, 7013-492. That concerned me so I asked Matt to do a similar example as I watched. When he needed to "borrow" (he couldn't subtract the nine from the one), he crossed out the seven, wrote a six, then made the one into an eleven, skipping the hundred's place. Bingo! It was obvious to me that Matt didn't understand the base ten system. Now Matt was not dumb or slow. He'd been in good schools and supposedly was functioning at "grade level." But he was approaching math by rote, without understanding or searching for meaning.

Matt's lack of understanding is typical. I meet these children every year. It took two years to convince one student, Sarah, that math had form and purpose related to the real world. She had come to believe that she didn't need to think for math, she just needed to remember what someone told her to do.

Word problems as practice for even "easy" skills help students make a realistic connection between math at school and their lives. I use story problems not so much to sharpen problem solving skills as to convince a student of the relationship between math and life.

For Matt I begin with adding and subtracting money. I enlist a friend of Matt's who does understand the base ten system and get out my container of real money. (Yes, real money. It is significantly more motivating than play money. Fifth grade boys will not "play" with play

> "The teacher pretended that algebra was a perfectly natural affair, to be taken for granted, whereas I didn't even know what numbers were. . . Mathematics classes became sheer terror and torture to me. I was so intimidated by my incomprehension that I did not dare to ask any questions."
>
> —*Carl Jung*

money. Yes, sometimes I've lost some of my real money. But then, I haven't spent my real money on play money which also can get lost.) The standard procedure for using real money in my classroom is to first count the container and write down the amount they've received. In this case I give the boys five $1 bills, fifteen dimes and fifteen pennies. I don't include nickels and quarters because I'm emphasizing the ten system.

I model the teaching process so Matt's friend can help him learn. I explain, "Always start with some easy, warm up problems like 82¢ plus 16¢ or $1.43 plus $3.22. Remember, you are the teacher so you have to pre-think the problem to understand how hard it is. These problems don't have any carrying. What's another example without carrying?" I pause and check for his understanding. Matt is the target of this lesson but his friend's brain will be turned on and tuned in as he teaches. There are benefits for both children, besides the enjoyment of working together.

I ask Matt's friend to write down his problems on paper using the regular format of dollar sign and decimal, but to also write it plain, without reference to money ($3.21 + $1.27= ___, and 321 + 127= ___). I continue teaching and model problems with zeros as place holders using both addition and subtraction. This really doesn't take very long because Matt's friend understands the math, it's just the teaching steps he is learning. Within five minutes the two boys are working together, first with the teacher making the written record of the problems then with Matt recording his work on paper, in both forms, while he's using the money. This activity "counts for a page of math" for both of the boys. They to turn in their activity record sheet to "get credit".

The next day I spend a few minutes working with Matt using the Base Ten blocks.[3] I began by using money because Matt's more familiar with it. Now the Base Ten blocks make sense and I am able to use larger numbers than I could with classroom money. Again I begin with something easy, 305-182 but quickly am able to move to 2007-245. As Matt trades the blocks the base ten system begins to dawn on him. He starts to understand what he's doing and why. He's on his way. (Matt didn't need extensive re-teaching but some children do. I use *Understanding Place Value*[4] reproducible activity pages when a child needs significant repetition.)

A few days later I show Matt a sample page of story problems using addition and subtraction with large numbers. I ask Matt to make up his own math page with ten story problems for subtraction using numbers from 999 to 99,999. "Think about how we use numbers in real life. Figure out the answers but write them on another sheet of paper. We'll give your problems to someone else to solve." Of course this work also "counts" as a math page.

In a week's time Matt has been able to internalize our base ten system. I started with easy work grounded in money which he already knew. His friend helped him but it didn't make Matt feel dumb because everyone in our room is working on different things. Students' differences are respected. Matt feels good about himself and the "correction" process was interesting rather than a punishment.

I teach all math concepts with this basic process. I begin with what is already known. I help students take mini-steps to build a concept, then transfer the concept to other materials. I use story problems to enclose the math concept in real life situations.

-∞-

Many teachers understand the importance of having children build models of the multiplication tables. Students internalize three groups of seven as they lay out seven tiles[1] in a row, and then make three rows. It is important that students do the reverse also: twenty-one tiles arranged in three rows have seven in each row. All four members of the "family of facts" should be practiced until readily apparent to each student, i.e. 3 groups of 7 = 21, 7 groups of 3 = 21, 21 divided into 3 groups = 7 in a group, 21 divided into 7 groups = 3 in a group (3 times 7 = 21, 7 times 3 = 21, 21 divided by 3 = 7, 21 divided by 7 = 3).

More complicated multiplication and division can be shown in much the same manner using Base Ten blocks. It is possible to build 14 x 12 just as you can build 3 x 7 by using manipulatives. Students need to use their visual and their tactile/kinesthetic senses while verbalizing the concepts. *Understanding Place Value: Multiplication and Division* provides both teacher explanations and student activity pages to practice larger multiplication/division computation using Base Ten blocks.[6]

When I begin to teach fractions I ask students to recall examples of having only part of something, like pizza or brownies. Then I use fraction circles[7] because it's obvious when there is a whole. I work with children in small groups so I'm sure students are successfully manipulating the pieces as they verbalize concepts. I don't want anyone to practice wrong.

We spend a few days identifying fractional parts with the corresponding mathematical symbols (1/4, 3/5). And, I encourage students to play around with ways to make a whole circle.

We begin to add fourths, then eighths. We work with common denominator fractions until they become automatic. Then I throw in a simple problem with uncommon denominators and the fun begins. (A discrepant event perks up the brain. The established pattern of understanding is threatened and new thinking is stimulated.) Rather than giving a formula I want my students to experiment with the uncommon denominator dilemma. Finally after days of matching and trading pieces in order to find common denominators, I ask if anyone wants to know how to do it without having to use the circle pieces. I've set the stage with the discrepant event; my students have experienced the fractions thoroughly, and now I discuss how to find the Greatest Common Multiple.

Mathematical manipulation of fractions is a very abstract thinking process. Once my students are efficient at using the fraction circles and have begun to understand the algorithm, I switch the physical materials to fraction strips[8] or fractional pattern block problems. For some students the change in materials completely throws off their thinking (which is exactly why it's important to use different materials). The concept of parts and whole hasn't become independently constructed in their thoughts; they are tied to the circles. In time, fraction concepts transfer to different materials easily, but it takes time and experiences.

Dennis the Menace is smelling the aroma of a mouth-watering pizza as his mother begins to slice it, "Cut it up into a LOT of slices, Mom. I'm really hungry!"

-∞-

I teach decimals by beginning with our money system, using dollars, dimes and pennies. Later I use the Base Ten "hundred square" blocks turned upside down (no demarcations of ones but rather the smooth side), with the ten sticks to represents tenths and the small cubes representing hundredths.

The process is repeated: connect to prior knowledge, introduce new ideas in the simplest possible way, transfer ideas to another medium, use the ideas in story problems, then have students make up their own story problems.[9]

After students have a working understanding of decimals it's fun to do complicated calculator work. Children love the giant numbers and multi-step calculations. As we begin I re-teach problem solving strategies — guess and check, do a simpler problem, make a table or picture, act it out, make a list, figure out patterns, or work backwards. There are quite a few good resources on calculator story problems.[10]

This kind of computational math learning happens during my morning work time. Some students are working on multiplication while others are using calculators. Everyone is working "hard enough but not too hard".

Some students are working alone; others with a partner or small group. I am busy teaching small groups or consulting with an individual. I have not assigned each student specific practice pages; students choose their own pages. Choice is important. I want my students to understand what they need to learn, seek out the explanation from one of my teaching groups or a friend, and then practice until the concept is easy. I have prepared sheets on a wide variety of math topics. Most of these pages are self correcting, thus guarding against practicing wrong.[11]

One day found Buddy working on division while Brian was working on calculator pages. Elizabeth and Alexa had chosen to work on rounding decimals. About six students are working on a fraction page I just modelled on the chalkboard. My expectation is four math practice pages a week, but a practice page may include a math reinforcement game such as my homemade "Decimal In-Between" or the commercial "Twenty-Four Game".[12] On occasion a student turns in a paper which I suspect is too easy. I confer with the child asking, "Was this work hard enough? I thought you knew this, am I wrong?" Sometimes I accept the explanation; other times we agree to disregard the work.

"Holding people to the responsible course is not demeaning, it is affirming"
—*Stephen Covey*

There are many other math activities happening in my class through the year. When I emphasize linear measurement I set up a table with meter sticks, yardsticks, tape measures and 12 inch rulers. Activity sheets are there to be picked up to guide measuring activities inside and outside our classroom.

Another time containers for liquid measurement, in both standard and metric sizes, are set by a water table. An assignment will define minimum expectations, but students can and do "mess with" the containers as much as they like.

I use Venn diagrams whenever appropriate through the school year, as well as "What's My Rule?" strategies in our math maintenance routine.

We create 3-D geometric shapes from 2-D patterns. We create tessellations and curve stitch designs.[13] We graph four quadrant coordinates and enlarge simple pictures by enlarging the quadrants. We explore mobius strips and flexa-hexagons. We play spatial games like Othello and take on challenges like the Tower of Hanoi.

Cooperative TEAMs work on probability projects, the *Equals Get It Together* collection of problem-solving situations[14] and *Puzzlegrams*[15], a wonderful book which a former student gave me.

Math in my classroom stimulates logical-mathematical intelligence and visual-spatial intelligence while using linguistic and interpersonal intelligences. Math skill lessons are taught only to students who need them. Math thinking lessons are usually done with cooperative groups. Fascinating math experiences, like mobius strips, are presented to the whole group. Sometimes children come into my class disliking math or feeling a lack of confidence, but they don't leave me that way. Math is fun and math is diverse. Math means a lot of different things and I enjoy helping children become intrigued by math's many dimensions.

∞

[1] Two excellent sources of math materials are Creative Publications (800-624-0822) and Dale Seymour Publications (800-872-1100). Call for their catalog. Unless otherwise noted, the materials I use come from these catalogs.

[2] The Hands-On Equations Learning System, Borenson and Associates, P.O. Box 3328, Allentown, PA 18106.

[3] These Base Ten blocks are available from Creative Publications.

[4] *Understanding Place Value* available from Creative Publications, $23.50.

[5] I use inch ceramic tiles left over from a remodelling project. If you put a note out to the school's parents I bet you can get some free. Otherwise ask a tile store to donate some for a tax write-off.

[6] *Understanding Place Value.*

[7] My circles are homemade — different colored construction paper laminates. Creative Publications sells plastic pieces for only $10. They

also sell a number of activity books and sets of "jobcards" which are excellent.

[8] Fraction Strips, Dale Seymour.

[9] WorkMat Math: *Thinking Through Story Problems and Story Problems on Their Own*, Creative Publications. Also the TOPS materials (Techniques of Problem Solving), Dale Seymour.

[10] I have used the TOPS Calculator Problem Decks (one box of 200 problem cards for each grade level 3-6) from Dale Seymour and *The Problem Solver with Calculators* designed from grades 4-8th, Creative Publications.

[11] Creative Publications has a series of five *"Math With Pizzazz!"* reproducible notebooks covering topics from basic facts to pre-algebra. Each is self-corrected as the student works the problems by decoding a pun or riddle. This makes an individualized math program much easier to set up and keep track of.

[12] Dale Seymour sells it for $14.50, but I've seen it in a drug store for about $5.00.

[13] Dale Seymour has books on both topics.

[14] I use ideas from the Middle Grades Mathematics Projects book on *Probability*, published by Addison-Wesley which is $3.95, and *Equals Get It Together*, $15.00, both from Dale Seymour.

[15] *Puzzlegrams* (Simon & Schuster:1989).

Learning to Learn

11

Goal setting ... Affirmations ... Choices ... Self-evaluation ... Study habits ... Memorizing ...
Perennial wisdom ... Daily plans ... Service learning ... It's essential.

Success for every child is the goal. Somehow along the way an important but often invisible ingredient must be added. Robert Sternberg calls it practical intelligence. Others may call it learning how to learn. It has to do with managing oneself, dealing with schedules, understanding how to study, and getting things done.

Understanding one's learning style is part of this process. Being able to set goals, coping with time deadlines, and making good choices about learning environments and learning strategies are also part of the process. Knowing ways to generate creative thoughts, how to approach a textbook, take notes, memorize, and evaluate what's important are also necessary skills. Identifying patterns and relationships, planning projects, staying organized and preparing for tests are also crucial ingredients of practical intelligence. Too often these skills are left to chance, yet they are the underpinnings of learning. I do not leave these skills to chance. I directly teach these learning strategies and plan ways for my students to practice them.

Our September goal setting process leads naturally to a group discussion of goals. Children in our school have a sense of goals because of their involvement in these conferences, but they need to apply goal-seeking skills to others areas of their lives.

I begin the discussion. "Think of a goal you have had recently. It may have been in sports, or music, or saving some money to buy something special. Who will share their goal?" Students readily give examples. Then I ask, "Why set a goal for yourself?" I create a web on the chalkboard with "Why Goals?" in the center and attach the flow of ideas from the students.

As the flow of ideas begin to wane, I share a quote from Elinor Smith, a pioneer aviator.

"It had long since come to my attention that people of accomplishment rarely sat back and let things happen to them. They went out and happened to things." I ask if the children know any other sayings about goals and elicit other ideas.

Thinking about what you are trying to accomplish is a basic life-long skill. Two processes help plant the seeds of success — affirmations and imagery. Both effect the non-verbal right hemisphere, our "subconscious" readiness to be successful.

Affirmations are stated in the positive personal present. "I am turning my work in on time." (Rather than "I'm going to turn in my work on time.) "I am concentrating easily because I choose a wise place to work." (Rather than "I'm not going to sit with my friends and talk when I have work to do.")[1]

The brain has no picture for the negative, only the action. When someone says, "Don't throw rocks on the playground," the brain has to picture throwing rocks and tell itself not to. But, in fact, the visual picture was throwing rocks. That's why it is important to focus on positive imagery and directions.

We all have heard children say "I can't". When I hear a student say I can't I respond with a gentle rephrase, "You mean you haven't learned it yet. Are you finished learning everything?" It's easy to forget that none of us is finished learning and growing. Affirmations help change "I can't" to positive self-talk of "I can."

Children naturally pretend in order to learn. They express what they understand by using their imaginations to role play situations. Children pretend to be mommies and daddies. They pretend to be doctors. Traditional Native children pretended to be scouts. They emulated the behaviors of older respected people. They learned by practicing. I ask children to pretend to be successful at their goals. "Think about a goal you are working on this week. Pretend that you just succeeded in completing that goal. In your imagination, see yourself completing the goal. It may be running really fast or finishing your project. Think clearly about your goal then imagine how great it feels to complete your goal. Feel the pride in your stomach. Feel the smile on your face. Notice the other people who are proud of you — it may be your mom or dad, it may be me or another teacher at school. Your friends may be proud of you also. Feel how good it feels, enjoy your accomplishment. You set a goal and you did it!"[2]

"Schools can no longer function as filling stations to which young people drive up, receive the knowledge they need for a working lifetime, and then drive away. Students must be taught to think and solve problems. The new goal of education is to learn to learn."
— *Edward Fiske,*
Smart Schools, Smart Kids

Two time pentathlete Marilyn King states "To accomplish any lofty goal you must have a crystal clear image of that goal and keep it uppermost in your mind. We know that by maintaining that image, the "how-to" steps necessary for the realization of the goal will begin to emerge spontaneously. If you cannot imagine the goal, the "how-to" steps will never emerge, and you'll never do it. Clearly the first step to any achievements is to dare to imagine that you can do it."

— "Ordinary Olympians,"
In Context, #18 (Winter 1988)

Another time I ask students to focus on a goal. Note that I'm asking children to focus on one specific goal at a time. I'll talk them through imagining their success and then ask them to paint the picture vividly and clearly in their heads. Then I'll make an assignment to draw their success in full color. These techniques also work for adults to accomplish their goals.[3]

Goal setting and affirmations are positive choices that promote growth. Too often children have not been told they can or do make choices. It is important to directly teach children about choices. The greater the awareness of choices and their implications, the greater the sense of control.

Last year our school emphasized the importance of choices through our theme "Changes, Choices, Challenges." Such a theme can be used in any classroom as a helpful lens to focus thinking. I began the theme by brainstorming about change, asking students to catalog things they see changing. We change, feelings change, the environment changes, the earth changes. Essentially, everything all around us is constantly changing.

A week later I suggested, "If everything is changing, what are our choices?" We began webbing some choices students had made so far that day. Then switched to choices at school. As a staff we believe children learn to make good choices by making choices. Thus, we allow many choices each day, discussing alternatives so students don't make the choices too casually.

Daily I link thinking about actions and choices. "What assignment do you choose to start on?" "Is it a good choice to work alone or work with a friend to practice your spelling?" "Knowing your learning style, what is your choice of the best homework environment?" "Why did you choose to solve the math problem with this chart?" "If you choose to settle down right away there will be more time for sharing." "How will you choose to set up a table to collect your science data?" My point is simply that when we stop to realize we have a choice and evaluate how we want to proceed, we are more thoughtful. Believing you have a choice leads to conscious decision making. Making decisions enhances the self control or self power an individual feels.

Making choices leads the way to active self evaluation. Evaluation is a critical part of success — choose a plan — do the plan — then evaluate. This constant thoughtful feedback circle leads to high quality thinking and products.

Throughout this book I have shared a number of ways to help students learn self-evaluation habits: scale of 1-5 on fingers, self-evaluation of goals, evaluating other students' reports, asking for feedback on writing projects, saving and culling portfolios, as well as making daily activity plans. In any thoughtful process of helping students "learn to learn" it is necessary to learn to think about what you have just done, pat yourself on the back for doing a good job and think about other ways you may have done it more easily or better. Reflective evaluation needs to become an internal habit and friend.

Another important item to evaluate is study habits. Different strokes are for different folks when it comes to study habits, because of different learning styles. One person needs silence and a desk, another actually focuses best relaxing on their bed with some background music. To think about study habits, and to evaluate if students are making appropriate choices, I have my students take their learning styles inventories out of their portfolios to review. Students need to understand if they learn best with auditory, visual or tactile/kinesthetic stimulus. And it's important for each learner to know if she learns best by discussing information and quizzing each other in a study group, or by working alone. Time of day, intake, global or analytic style, and all of the other learning style factors impact learning.[4] Ken Dunn has developed a new audio-video, multi-cultural rap for high school students. The *Personal Learning Power* music video is part of the *Amazing Grades* materials explaining how to improve your grades by respecting your learning style.[5] Discussing study habits helps students evaluate what is most effective and encourages them to make good choices.

Often children, and their parents, have the belief that studying means sitting still for long periods of time to really concentrate. Fortunately that isn't how our brains prefer it. The brain has on and off cycles rather than full speed ahead at all times. A 90 minute study time is effective for most people. Ten-minute segments of concentrated study should be followed with a short break. On the breaks it's good to get up, move around, stretch or snack, whatever is physical rather than mental. This break helps your brain digest and incubate what you studied. After 90 minutes it's good to give yourself a reward of a 15 minute break to relax.

"Much school-based assessment actually prevents students from becoming thoughtful respondents to, and judges of, their own work. The 'surprise' nature of many test items, the emphasis on objective knowledge, the once-over and one-time nature of most exams — all offer students lessons that are destructive to their capacity to thoughtfully judge their own work: (1) assessment comes from without, it is not a personal responsibility; (2) what matters is not the full range of your intuitions and knowledge but your performance on the slice of skills that appear on the test; (3) first draft work is good enough; and (4) achievement matters to the exclusion of development."

— *Dennie Palmer Wolf,*
Harvard's Project Zero

Although I don't encourage the use of textbooks, I do help students learn how to approach a text. Understanding the big picture is the first step. Students do this by paging through the material looking at the headings and the pictures. As they page I ask them to do some guessing about what the information is about. "Ask yourself some questions about how the material relates to things you already know. Look at any questions or review sections at the end of a chapter. You're trying to get a feel for what will be covered and consider connections you can make. Then go back and begin reading. Engage the brain while reading, ask yourself where the information is going and how it relates to your previous knowledge. Translate the information into pictures in your imagination. Select important points to underline if the book is yours (I hope you are underlining or highlighting this book). Otherwise take notes. Your note-taking style may be a traditional outline, it may be webbing and clustering with words, or you may learn best by combining quick sketches and doodles with a few words in a mind mapping style."[6]

Memorizing information is very different from understanding information. I believe it is better to understand and build a knowledge base by relating new material to other concepts which a student knows. But, I also know students will be expected to memorize at times so I share some strategies that can help them memorize more quickly. "First try to link the information to be memorized to other things you know. Make as many associations as possible. Search for patterns and categories. When you need to memorize something new, review it for ten minutes an hour that day, then review five minutes the next day, and five minutes the next week. Continue reviewing for five minutes with longer time spans between. The worst thing to do is to read material and then put it aside for a week or two. It's important to use as many modalities as possible while memorizing. Walk around while you review. Use the material in a rap. Visualize about the information, or draw about it. Make a 3-D project about the material." There are systems of word association, like linking words to outrageous mental images, which students can learn if they are expected to memorize lists.[7] These techniques take some practice before they are effective memory organizers.

Understanding how we remember helps us understand students' thinking. The first key to memory is attention. The RAS and the Limbic System regulate the brain's attention. Two structures in the Limbic

System directly affect memory. The amygdala associates events with emotions. Can you remember where you were and what you were doing when the Gulf War began? Can you remember what you were doing at the same time the day before? Events which are impacted by emotions are most easily remembered. The hippocampus receives information from all the sensory systems. The wider the involvement of multiple sensory systems, the more stimulating the experience, and the more attention it receives, the more memory is increased. Finally, the more links or connections an experience has to other experiences or knowledge, the easier it is to remember. Developmentally appropriate experiences engage more brain power because more mind maps can process the experience.

Long term memories are not located in a particular place in the brain. I have no neurons which remember my grandmother's face. Current research and thinking about the brain suggest that memory is not a matter of storage and retrieval, but a dynamic process of categorizing and recategorizing sensory experiences.

"Memory," writes Israel Rosenfield in *The Invention of Memory*, "is not an exact repetition of an image in one's brain, but a recategorization. Recategorizations occur when the connections between the neuronal groups in different maps are temporarily strengthened. Recategorization of objects or events depends on motion as well as sensation, and it is a skill acquired in the course of experience. We do not simply store images or bits, but become more richly endowed with the capacity to categorize in connected ways."[8]

Gerald Edelman, director of The Neurosciences Institute at The Rockefeller University in New York states it another way, "Remembering is not the re-excitation of innumerable fixed, lifeless and fragmentary traces. It is an imaginative reconstruction, or construction, built out of the relation of our attitude towards a whole active mass of organized past reactions or experience, and to a little outstanding detail which commonly appears in image or in language form."[9] Rosenfield believes human intelligence is not simply knowing more, but rather the process of "reworking, recategorizing, and thus generalizing information in new and surprising ways."[10]

In my classroom I want students to remember as much as possible, as easily as possible. To foster memory I emphasize positive emotions,

"All right Buddy! You really improved your multiplication facts timing, good going!" I constantly link experiences to students' prior knowledge, spending plenty of time developing the Quadrant One, Anticipatory Set connections (the first step in Bernice McCarthy's *4MAT* System that was introduced in chapter 3). I use metaphors, "How is this problem like . . ." to help students make connections. I use multi-sensory experiences which are interesting to my students. I connect concepts within themes. I do not expect students to remember isolated facts but rather facts embedded within concepts, rich in experience.

Memories are "state-bound". That is, they are always linked to the entire physical and emotional environment in which they were experienced. Therefore it's best to study for a morning test in the morning. Its best to study in a calm and relaxed state, if you want to be calm and relaxed during the test. Unfortunately facts memorized for a test are bound to a test-state and are often not easily retrieved for real-life thinking.

-∞-

I believe another part of tacit knowledge is learning positive attitudes toward life. I purposely include time to discuss important thoughts of perennial wisdom each morning. We begin our day in a class meeting and, along with attendance and lunch count, we read the thought for the day. I use many ideas from the book, *Making the Most of Today*.[11] Like an AA book in its style, it encapsulates simple good wisdom for young people in pithy phrases and sayings. Thoughts like "Being under stress is like being inside a ball of rubber bands" (Earl Hipp) or "To escape criticism — do nothing, say nothing, be nothing" (Elbert Hubbard) lead to powerful and important discussions among students. After the thought there is a short paragraph of discussion and then an affirmation like, "Today I'll appreciate people for who and what they are".

After this daily routine, I help the children understand the flow of our day. Two lists are on our chalkboard to help my students plan. The first is a weekly assignment list (First draft of "Conversation Story" due Tuesday, Spelling due Thursday, leaf drawing due Friday, etc.). Each week I make a point of having assignments which require different skills or intelligences, not just traditional tasks. The other list keeps track of important dates in the next month (MLK assembly on Jan. 10, Note cards due on Jan. 14, Museum Jan. 25). Both lists help children plan their lives, know what to expect and what's going to be happening. As I am about to dismiss the students from our morning meeting I ask, "Scale of 1-5 how close are you to being done with your note cards?" "Tell two people what your morning plan is." Or, "How is a rubber band like your work today?" Metaphors stretch connection-making and deepen thought. All of the thoughts help my students to focus on their tasks and make conscious decisons about their activities in the next few hours.

-∞-

There are several learning to learn programs available to educators. Robert Sternberg and Howard Gardner have collaborated on a middle school curriculum, *Practical Intelligence for Schools* (PIFS).[12] which I have used many times in my class. There are three units formatted into 48 lessons. The first unit on "Managing Yourself" introduces Gardner's multiple intelligences and Sternberg's triarchic theory of intelligence. The curricular activities enable students to identify the strengths and weaknesses of their skills in the different areas with a checklist of examples for each intelligence. Students are helped to understand their own strengths and to appreciate other students' strengths. This unit is an important tool in enabling students and teachers to broaden their understanding of intelligence.

The second section of PIFS, "Managing Yourself", deals with learning styles. Student lessons are presented to teach perceptual modalities, the Dunns' system and to "whole and parts" processing, also known as global and analytic processing.

The last section discusses "Improving Your Own Learning". It stresses the importance of connecting information to prior knowledge. Lessons include memory strategies and the importance of visual imagery. The unit also provides strategies for improving listening, engaging all perceptual modalities, and setting short and long term goals.

The second unit is titled "Managing Tasks". It begins by providing student practice in identifying problems and planning to deal with, or prevent, problems. Then the curriculum examines specific study strategies such as note taking, finding the main idea, idea mapping or outlining, understanding the difference between literal and inferential questions, and taking tests. I have used numerous lessons in this section with students successfully.

The final unit, "Cooperating with Others" deals with communication skills and fitting into school. Many of the premises of cooperative learning are developed in these student activities, followed by sections on making choices and understanding the overall school system.

Sternberg believes directly teaching these skills is very important. In the past some students picked up these skills by happenstance, some never at all.

-∞-

Service-learning[13] is another important aspect of Learning to Learn. Children derive many benefits from lending their talents to better the community. Within our building students help adults, help other students and are in leadership roles in our Student Council. Many places in our school function better because students volunteer to help. Each Fall the Barton staff completes a survey of possible student jobs. Our Student Council Health and Welfare Secretaries publicize the school's needs and the skills required for student applicants. Interested students apply and interview directly with the adult requesting help.

Other service-learning happens directly with children. Children are mentors to other children in a number of ways. My classroom and other middle rooms pair up with a younger room for a year-long relationship. Twice a week for a half hour my students work with first and second graders. Some of the younger students need tutoring help with "basic skills" and some need mentoring beyond the "normal" expectations of skill levels. Each of my students need to plan for the younger student. Some of my students don't do a great job planning, but they sure establish important relationships with the younger child. Some other students in my room work extensively on their plans only to find the younger child did not cooperate. In my mind I say, "Welcome to the real world of teaching." But externally I help my students reflect, "What worked and what didn't seem to work?" "Do you think you know why she cooperated with that?" "How would you plan it differently next time?"

Students may also participate in service-learning experiences which reach beyond our school building. Our student council sponsors a collection of canned goods for a food shelf. One classroom helps serve at a "soup kitchen". Another has established a relationship with a nursing home and the nearby day care center. Some classes clean our local park while another lobbies for environmental issues. The number of ways to get involved in the community are as varied and rich as the students and staff conceiving the project.

The benefits of service-learning connect to practical intelligence, interpersonal intelligence and intrapersonal intelligence. The final chapter of *Reclaiming Youth at Risk*, an excellent book which examines the alienation of Native American students and principles of "creating reclaiming environments", focuses on service-learning. The book notes Diane Hedin's studies which indicate service-learning can "motivate youth who are bored with school by linking academic learning with real human needs; increase achievement for youth working as volunteer peer tutors; increase problem solving skills; and develop more complex patterns of thinking."[14]

Service-learning, whether in the school community or the broader community, has a component beyond simply volunteering. That component is added when adults help the students to reflect and learn from the experience. These adults guide students by initiating journal entries and discussions of their service experiences. The process enhances students' self-evaluations and highlights their contributions.

Learning to learn is essential. Students need to develop habits which promote lifelong learning for tomorrow's world. Anything less is a disservice to our children. While some students are able to pick up these skills at home, directly teaching the skills allow all students success. Leaving "learning to learn" skills to chance effectively discriminates against students without the home support to provide these insights.

∞

[1] For further reading see Jerry Fankhouser, *The Power of Affirmations* (Coleman Graphics: 1983), or Launa Ellison "Positive Self Talk," *Teaching K-8*, August/September 1987, p. 80.

[2] Other resources: Lane Longino Waas, *Imagine That!* (Jalmar Press: 1991), a good overview of the use of imagery and many imagery scripts linked to the seven intelligences. Richard de Mille's *Put Your Mother on the Ceiling* (Viking Press: 1973), is set up as mental games. It helps to focus and stretch the imagination of children.

[3] Adult books on using imagery are Adelaide Bry, *Visualization, Directing the Movies of Your Mind* (Harper & Row: 1978), Arnold Lazarus, *In*

the *Mind's Eye, The Power of Imagery for Personal Enrichment* (Guilford Press: 1977), and Patrick Fanning, *Visualization for Change* (New Harbinger: 1988).

[4] One resource for 5 - 8th graders is Tobias and Guild's *No Sweat, How to Use Your Learning Style To Be a Better Student.* ($5.95 from The Teaching Advisory, P.O. Box 99131, Seattle, WA 98199).

[5] *Amazing Grades* program includes 15 minute musical video teaching the Dunn factors of learning styles, hour audio cassette discussion of factors and the test, and four short workbooks. For information contact, Great Ocean Publishers, 703-525-0909. Meant for individual use but applicable to classes (5 - college).

[6] Nancy Margulies, *Mapping Inner Space, Learning and Teaching Mind Mapping* (Zephyr Press, $21.95). This can be a very effective way to remember information and you really do not have to be an artist to do it.

[7] Tony Buzan, *Use Both Sides Of Your Brain* (E.P. Dutton: 1976), Kline and Martel, *School Success* (Great Ocean Publishers: 1992), or Susan Barrett, *It's All in Your Head* (Free Spirit Publishing: 1985).

[8] Israel Rosenfield, *The Invention of Memory* (Basic Books: 1988), p. 192.

[9] *Ibid.*, p. 193.

[10] *Ibid.*, p. 193.

[11] Pamela Espeland and Rosemary Wallner, *Making the Most of Today* (Free Spirit Publishing: 1991). Appropriate for ten years old and older.

[12] *Practical Intelligence for Schools* (PIFS), Robert Sternberg, Yale University Dept. of Psychology, Box 11 A Yale Station, New Haven, CT 06520-7447. Student Text-$15., Teacher's Manual $35.

[13] Resources include Rich Cairn and James Kielsmeier, *Growing Hope: A Sourcebook on Integrating Youth Service into the School Curriculum* (National Youth Leadership Council: 1991). This sourcebook of what's really happened and how to do it is available from NYLC, 1910 West County Road B, Roseville, MN 55113. Barbara Lewis, *The Kid's Guide to Social Action* (Free Spirit Publishing: 1991), everything kid's need to take on a cause and change how it's being handled by adults. Kathy Henderson, *What Would We Do Without You? A Guide to Volunteer Activities for Kids* (Betterway Publications: 1990), a warm explanation of whom preteens and teens can help — the young, the old, the animals, the museums and more.

[14] Larry Brendtro, Martin Brokenleg and Steve Van Bockern, *Reclaiming Youth At Risk: Our Hope for the Future* (National Education Service: 1990), p. 92.

What You Can Do
Until The Revolution Comes
To Your School

12

A review ... Taking steps ... The final test.

There are a number of educational issues which have pulled at my heartstrings, pushing me to birth this book. My purpose, first and foremost, is to increase an understanding of the brain's role in learning. Educators are mostly unaware of the mechanism of learning, the basic hardware of the human brain. Years of technological research have yielded a clearer picture of the underlying principles which mold our thinking. Each living organism has its rules. The rules for nurturing growth in cactus are different from nurturing the growth of water lilies, but clearly there are rules. The rules for nurturing brains' growth have become increasingly clear.

Seeing With Magic Glasses is a wake-up call. The brain does have something to do with learning; basic principles must be respected so students can learn more.

Wise observers intuitively understood many of these neurological principles before brain researchers "proved" them. Maslow distinguished a hierarchy of needs and Piaget recognized the stages of childhood development. Others contributed important educational insights. In the sixties I read Sylvia Ashton-Warner's *Teacher*.[1] Her sense of respectful patience as she "taught" organic language resonates in my memory. In the seventies I read Carl Rogers' *Freedom to Learn*.[2] Many elements of his model of change, a model to reshape education, are now understood to be elements of brain-compatible education.

I began my teaching career hearing these writers' voices during my evenings' reflections yet I was experiencing a different reality daily in school. Rogers' message was clear: children are natural learners; take away threats; connect to what children already know; start where they are; enrich children's sensory experiences; involve feeling as well as intellect; stimulate creativity, self-reliance and independence; encourage self-evaluation. I tried but I shied away.

"Every era opens with its challenges, and they cannot be met by elaborating methods of the past."

— *Charles Lindbergh*

"The key to being a more effective educator, therefore, is not simply to find a specific methodology or technique. It is to grasp what actually happens in the brain during learning and to appreciate how all the different components of experience work together to help the brain do its job. The task, then, is for educators to deeply understand the way in which the brain learns. The more profound the understanding, the easier it is to actually see what is happening in a classroom and to creatively introduce the necessary changes."

— *Caine and Caine*

So many "experienced" teachers were using strict discipline to control children. I was a beginning teacher; what did I know. But I knew. I knew respect rather than control would free the learner.

In the eighties I read Leslie Hart.[3] With clarion voice he proclaimed the relevance of the Triune Brain theory in the classroom, realizing that threat leads to impaired learning because of the Reptilian "fight or flight" system. Hart spoke of the brain's need for extensive sensory stimulation, thus giving the brain enough input to detect patterns and create programs to handle typical situations.

I read the brain researchers, Roger Sperry, Michael Gazzaniga, Jere Levy, Geschwind and Galaburda, and Richard Restak. And, as I taught children each day, the children taught me. I began to link these scientific discoveries to what my students were doing.

The three pound universe, as one author has labelled the brain, is a marvelously complex organism which creates itself in relationship to its environment, yet it has rules. It will function best without threat. Relaxation of the body encourages better brain work. Cooperation and positive social interaction promote a safe environment. Mistakes are valuable for re-direction provided the environment remains safe.

Each brain is unique. The uniqueness, in part, is a combination of how the personality and various learning style factors interact with the external environment.

The brain constructs concepts by utilizing sensory stimulation and connecting it to prior knowledge, organizing information into meaningful patterns and programs. A thematic curriculum facilitates learning by aiding the connection making process of identifying patterns and relationships.

Developmentally, thinking is promoted by the processes of myelination which readies neurons for effective action. The process of myelination flows in spurts and plateaus which seem to relate to Piaget's observable stages.

A more mature definition of intelligence includes a wide variety of thinking processes, rather then a narrow focus based on left hemisphere processing. Children, unique miracles of these intelligences, come to school with vastly different needs. A curriculum cannot define what a child needs. To foster children's learning teachers must do whatever it takes. Teachers must become skilled at observing what a child needs and finding ways to support the child in meeting these needs. There is no recipe, but my magic glasses help me to find the ingredients of each success. A teacher's role becomes highly creative in working with each child's needs. Parents play an important part furthering each child's total growth. Teachers must work with the whole child and parents are the key to the whole child picture.

Language and math, two subjects our society values greatly, must be developed with whole brain methods. Writing and drawing interface with play-making and problem-solving. Language supports math and math is integrally related to all of life. The teacher's role is to broaden an understanding of math, enriching our comfort as we interact with it.

Finally, there are many areas of tacit knowledge which need to be elucidated in our classrooms. Educators cannot afford to let the potential of some children slip away because they haven't been let into the secrets of working effectively. Learning to learn must become a priority for the education of all students. Learning how to study effectively, within your own learning style, is an essential element of success. Achieving habits of self-management, also essential, cannot be learned without practice. Practicing self-management means choices. It means that the teacher can not control the student with external force but rather must allow the student to practice, sometimes falling and getting up to begin again. Practice makes perfect, or rather it makes habits. If I want my students to have habits of goal-setting and self-evaluation I must let them practice. Practice, combined with self-evaluation, builds positive habits, the well worn pathways in one's brain. Positive self-management leads to effective independent thinking and that, in turn, is a link to a successful future, for the child and the larger world community.

∞

Stephen Covey in *The 7 Habits of Highly Effective People* poignantly states that "self-growth is tender; it's holy ground. There's no greater investment."[4] Your self growth as teacher facilitates the students' self-growth. And, as folk wisdom points out, a thousand mile journey begins with the first step. To determine your first step I encourage you to read this list and check the ideas which may, just may, be possible for you. You are unique. Your place in your personal life, your current

"Instruction begins when you, the teacher, learn from the learner; put yourself in his place so that you may understand what he learns and the way he understands it."
— *Kierkegaard*

"If I really want to improve my situation, I can work on the one thing over which I have control — myself."

— *Stephen Covey*

awareness of issues, the length you have taught at a particular grade level or in a particular school, and your environment are all factors in how you decide to begin. There isn't one entry point. The important point is your commitment to continue to grow, for your sake and for the sake of the children who will come down your path. Take just one step at a time. Make only one change at a time and stay with it until you, and your children, are comfortable with it. Then take just one more step.

-∞-

The WHAT YOU CAN DO TILL THE REVOLUTION COMES TO YOUR SCHOOL Checklist.

Part One: put a check on any ideas which may be possible for you.

__ Tell your students you believe they are smart. Tell them often.

__ Understand your personality type, and the personalities of those you love.

__ Understand your modality strengths and the strengths of those you love.

__ Understand the Dunn and Dunn factors that are important to you, and those important to those you love.

__ Discuss an aspect of learning styles with friends.

__ Subscribe to the Learning Style Network to keep abreast of research related to Dunn and Dunn's work.[5]

__ Subscribe to the Consortium for Whole Brain Learning for continual dialogue and information on new resources.[6]

__ When you use a new learning style idea in your classroom explain it to your students. Changes don't just happen, they are purposely created.

"The apparent rule is that when students are given meaningful choices in their education they are likely to learn more, for they are learning what they have elected to learn."

— *Purkey and Novak*

__ Reproduce relevant articles for your colleagues. Give them directly to people, or stick them in staff mail boxes anonymously, or simply leave them laying around in your office, workroom or teacher lunchroom.

__ Suggest your staff make time to discuss an idea in this book, or discuss an entire chapter.

__ Schedule a discussion on one of these ideas with parents: invite a speaker in, hold a parent-staff dialogue, create a vision, show the film *Why Do These Kids Love School?*[7]

__ Brainstorm ways you can help parents understand your vision. What vehicles can you use to help bring parents along the road to your vision?

__ List what you have the power to change all by yourself. List what you'd like to have your colleagues help you change. List what you need to work with your principal to change.

__ Plan curriculum which has students translating content into an "arts" form — drama, drawing, painting, poetry, sculpting, music. This allows students to synthesize new information creatively.

__ Make personal goal statement. Support these goals by writing and drawing what it would be like to have accomplished your goal.

__ Create affirmations about your goal.

__ Collect more manipulatives: cardboard pizza rounds to use to teach fractions, one inch tiles from the odds and ends at stores or remodeling projects, pennies/dimes/dollars, fossils, rocks, bones, general junk to sort and use for Venn diagrams, old machines to take apart, money from other countries, and plants to experiment on.

__ Shop garage sales to increase your classroom library and your supply of books for teaching groups. Enlist parents to find books also.

__ Begin using hand signals "On the scale of one to five . . ." for immediate feedback on students' self-evaluation.

__ Ask your students what feels good at school and what could be improved.

__ Work toward common expectations for student behavior in your school.

__ Invite parents in more often.

__ Send a monthly letter home to families to increase communication.

__ Begin to help students set goals.

__ Plan your class time in large blocks and allow students choice in what they work on when.

__ Teach TEAMwork and use it often.

__ Tell your students that you believe everyone can learn and you want everyone to learn.

"Change, of course, takes time. All learning is developmental, including the learning of educators."

— *Caine & Caine*

__ Expand the ways students can move around the room appropriately by setting up experiments and math activities which one or two children can work on at a time.

__ Plan a class theme for one month.

__ Use a guided imagery to stimulate creative writing.

__ Have students give each other feedback on their writing and rewrite it before its turned in to you.

__ Pair up with another class which is older or younger to help each other.

__ Have students create portfolios of their important work.

__ Share your students' portfolios with their parents.

— Survey the adults in your school for places students can help. Begin a service-learning project to help your school.

__ Work to strengthen student responsibility with Student Councils.

__ Post affirmations in your classroom.

__ Set aside a regular time for journals — for yourself and your students.

__ Teach yourself better relaxation methods, then when you get good at relaxing, teach a colleague and then your students.

__ Tell your students you want them to succeed. Tell them often!

__ Discuss why its important to ask questions, and make mistakes.

__ Teach your students about Gardner's theory of multiple intelligences.

__ Give students more choices, and help them evaluate their choices.

__ Contact the Lions Quest office for more information on the *Skills for Adolescence* or the *Skills for Growing* classes and materials.[8]

__ Order the "Generator", National Youth Leadership Council's *Journal of Service-Learning and Youth Leadership*.[9]

__ Buy one of the footnoted books, read it and discuss it.

__ Find others in your area who have tried some of these things and pick their brains.

__ Find others who want to try new things and start a regular scheduled support group.

__ Teach your students about the human brain.

__ Use music in your classroom to set the tone for activities.

__ Work with your students to make up raps to remember content.

__ Do more group problem solving activities.

__ Bring in some floor cushions to make a soft corner for reading and studying. Teach the students how to use the cushions.

"Good teaching cannot be reduced to a technique. Good teaching comes from the identity and integrity of the teacher."
— *Parker Palmer*

__ Ask your students if they ever get hungry at school. Explain the research on food intake and make a plan for snacks during class time.

__ Order interesting catalogues: Interact Simulations, Free Spirit Publishing, Great Ocean Publishers, Zephyr Press, Creative Publications, Dale Seymour.[10]

__ Clue your principal in on your professional development plan.

__ Write an article about learning styles for your newspaper.

__ Explain the Triune brain to your school board.

__ Collect quotes to use for a thought-of-the-day, or use *Making the Most of Today*.[11]

__ Strive to make each child's work "hard enough but not too hard".

__ Try using dots and checks to "correct" students writing so their work is left intact and they learn to proofread.

__ Work to get your school to designate a budget line item for learning style materials.

__ Be real with your students. Let them know you have sad days, bad days, joys and frustrations. You are an important role model for them.

__ Spend your energy building a new vision; don't put energy into tearing down the old, it will fade away as you create the new.

__ Teach "I statements" and use them yourself.[12]

__ Children need success every day, seek to find what they do well and affirm their success.

__ Teachers need success every day, seek to find what you have done well each day and affirm your success.

__ Remind students to relax so they can free greater brain power for use.

__ Vary students work settings — cooperative groups, pairs, individuals.

__ Spend class time generating multiple questions before searching for answers.

__ Reflect more on why students may be behaving as they are behaving.

__ Include all seven intelligences in each week's work through discussions, assignments and link to books, recess, sports, entertainment, etc.

__ Show respect for all cultural heritages by including their literature, important people and achievements; use in all content areas as a natural, not special, inclusion.

__ Strive to use multi-modalities for all input/output cycles.

"By working on ourselves instead of worrying about conditions, we were able to influence the conditions."
— *Stephen Covey*

__ Join with other teachers for a month's theme.

__ Work on a committee to plan a school wide yearly theme.

__ Begin a "Climate Committee" to work on positive attitudes and behavior in your schools. Climate includes all adults and students in the school.

__ Think of ways to use the arts each and every week (acting, miming, drawing, painting, constructing, singing, rapping, performing, dancing).

__ Take the time to connect to students' prior knowledge — always, for every child.

__ Return parents phone calls as soon as possible.

__ Plan a positive social skills program for your classroom.

__ Create clear behavior expectations. Teach them so students internalize them.

__ Reward appropriate behavior.

__ Smile a lot and get enough sleep so you can cope with younger energy.

__ Remember to greet your "Feelers" each day.

__ Plan lessons with personality type needs in mind.

__ Use a guided imagery to set the stage for a field trip.

__ Deliberately plan activities which go back and forth between the specialities of the hemispheres.

__ Choose an "at-risk" student and keep journal notes on what she does and what you think she may be feeling/thinking.

__ Take pictures of student activities and add them to the students' portfolios.

__ Start a plan to redesign your physical classroom. Bring in tables for common space and dividers for privacy.

__ Collect quotes which are powerful for you and share them with other adults in your school.

__ Imagine the success of every child. See it, hear it, feel it and rejoice.

__ Remember Goethe's wisdom, "Treat a man as he is and he will remain as he is. Treat a man (child) as he can and should be and he will become as he can and should be." Treat each child as if she or he has great contributions to make.

__ Act as if you are making important changes — you will.

∞

> "Can a profession whose charge is defined by the development of an effective and efficient human brain continue to remain uninformed about that brain?"
> — *Robert Sylwester*

> "Whether you think you can, or you think you can't, you are right."
> — *Henry Ford*

Part Two: Return to your check marks. Prioritize what you are able to do with ease, what you can take on yourself. Set some goals for yourself as well as dates to evaluate your progress.

-∞-

The final test is an example of authentic assessment. In the best sense a test should be a real evaluation of whether the information and concepts are internalized. An authentic assessment is real, rather than as Grant Wiggins says "a poor substitute" in the form of multiple choice questions.

The final test for this book happens as you return to this checklist in a month, or whatever personal date you set, for evaluation. The final test will be evidenced by the way you internalize these ideas and the way you use them in your classroom. You will be passing this test if these ideas become less strange and more approachable. You may choose to keep a portfolio, combining notes and photographs, or a journal to record your plans, feelings, triumphs and reflections. A journal or portfolio will help you congratulate yourself as you progress and document the journey.

Amelia Earhart said, "Everyone has her own Atlantic to fly. Whatever you want very much to do, against the opposition of tradition, neighborhood opinion, and so called common sense — that is an Atlantic."

Earhart's quote often sat near me as I paced and pounded the computer keys day after day. Writing this book was my Atlantic. Making the first steps toward teaching the brain's way may be your Atlantic. But, if we want children to grow we must grow. We must model the challenges and excitement of making changes and working toward new goals. We must be the lifelong learners we hope to help a younger generation to become. Oliver Wendell Holmes once said, "The human mind, once stretched to a new idea, never goes back to its original dimensions." I hope I have helped to stretch your mind. Thank you for sharing in my Atlantic. I hope my flight will encourage you to soar higher.

-∞-

[1] Sylvia Ashton-Warner, *Teacher* (Simon and Schuster: 1963).

[2] Carl Rogers, *Freedom to Learn* (Charles Merrill: 1969).

[3] Leslie Hart, *Human Brain and Human Learning* (Longman Inc.: 1983).

[4] Stephen Covey, *The 7 Habits of Highly Effective People* (Simon & Schuster: 1989), p. 62.

[5] Learning Style Network, St. John's University, Grand Central Pkwy., Jamaica NY 11439.

[6] Consortium for Whole Brain Learning, 3348 - 47th Ave. S., Mpls. MN 55406-2345.

[7] Dorothy Fadiman's award winning PBS special. Available from the Zephyr catalog among other places.

[8] Lions Quest office can be reached by calling 800-446-2700.

[9] "Generator", National Youth Leadership Council, 1910 West County Road B, Roseville, MN 55113. The $25.00 contribution is tax-deductible.

[10] Send postcards to request catalogs: Interact, P.O. Box 997-Y92, Lakeside, CA 92040; Free Spirit Publishing, 400 First Ave. N., Suite 616, Mpls., MN 55401-1724; Great Ocean Publishers, Inc., 1823 North Lincoln St., Arlington, VA 22207-3746 [SASE]; Zephyr Press, 3316 N. Chapel Ave., P.O. Box 13448-E, Tucson, AZ 857232-3448; Creative Publications, 5040 West 111th St., Oak Lawn, IL 60453, Dale Seymour Publications, P.O. Box 10888, Palo Alto, CA 94303-0879.

[11] Espeland and Wallner, *Making the Most of Today* (Free Spirit Publishing: 1991).

[12] Many sources have lessons of "I" statements, including the Lions Quest materials.

A Note on Terminology

I wrote this book without "educationese" — the technical phrases favored in current educational writing. However, for the readers who may appreciate such links, I offer this appendix.

Whole Language elements include the use of "real" literature instead of basal textbooks, writing as process instead of a one-time product, learning grammar while using it rather than worksheets, student choices and self-evaluation. The chapters on interdisciplinary themes and language model these concepts.

Constructionism is the process of each individual "constructing" concepts through experiences. Concepts do not become embedded in the brain simply by being told information. The chapters on thinking and math deal with constructionism.

Z.P.D. is an acronym for *Zone of Proximal Development*. It means "hard enough but not too hard." This theme repeats itself throughout the book beginning with the first chapter. It is a core concept of brain-wise teaching.

Total Quality refers to a process of continual self-evaluation and striving for improvement. It is a companion idea to "hard enough but not too hard." T.Q. means making a plan, doing it, evaluating what happened and making a new plan to begin the cycle again. It also means changing from a "boss teacher" to one who facilitates. It means eliminating fear and promoting trust and safety. I hope you have felt these points repeatedly through the book.

The *reflective teacher* is one who thinks about what is happening and plans strategies for improvement. It is linked to Total Quality ideas.

Authentic Assessment means evaluation without using an artificial mean, most often represented by tests. An authentic assessment of spelling is the students' daily written work. An authentic assessment of a group's understanding of the circulatory system is their class presentation. Student portfolios are also part of authentic assessment.

Mastery learning means success for everyone. In the best of worlds it means teaching so each student can learn, a recurring theme of this book. Mastery learning is the opposite of the bell curve which assumes an equal number of students will be unsuccessful as successful.

O.B.E. or *Outcome Based Education* means that the "authorities" expect certain outcomes, but the teachers and students can use any methods to achieve the outcome. These outcomes are broad — "communicate effectively" — and are demonstrated by authentic assessments. Thus, a sixth grader's well developed report on Amelia Earhart is a document which illustrates effective written communication. The accompanying presentation which entices other students to learn more illustrates effective oral communication. In my work with children I am consistently focused on the desired outcomes and use whatever it takes to get my students to achieve.

Bibliography / Resources

Aaronson, E. *The Jigsaw Classroom.* Beverly Hills, CA: Sage Publications, 1978.

Adderholdt-Elliott, Miriam. *Perfectionism: What's Bad About Being Too Good?* Minneapolis: Free Spirit Publishing, 1987.

Armstrong, Thomas. *Awakening Your Child's Natural Genius.* Los Angeles: Tarcher, 1991.

Armstrong, Thomas. *In Their Own Way.* Los Angeles: Tarcher, 1987.

Armstrong, Thomas. *7 Kinds of Smart.* New York: Penguin Books, 1993.

Ashton-Warner, Sylvia. *Teacher.* New York: Simon & Schuster, 1963.

Bandler, Richard. *Using Your Brain For A Change.* Moab, UT: Real People Press, 1985.

Barbe, Walter. *Growing Up Learning.* Washington, DC: Acropolis Books, 1985.

Barrett, Susan. *It's All in Your Head.* Minneapolis: Free Spirit Publishing, 1985. (Teacher's guide also available.)

Beck, Deva and James. *The Pleasure Connection: How Endorphins Affect Our Health and Happiness.* San Marcos, CA: Synthesis Press, 1987.

Benson, Herbert. *The Relaxation Response.* New York: William Morrow Co, 1975.

Belknap, Martha. *Taming Your Dragons.* Buffalo, NY: D.O.K. Publishers, 1990.

Bettelheim, Bruno and Karen Zelan. *On Learning to Read: The Child's Fascination with Meaning.* New York: Alfred Knopf, 1961.

Bloom, Lazerson and Hofstadter. *Brain, Mind and Behavior.* New York: Educational Broadcasting Corp., 1985.

Boughton, Simon. *Great Lives.* New York: Doubleday, 1989.

Bova, Ben. *The Weather Changes Man.* New York: Addison-Wesley, 1974.

Bowman-Kruhm, Mary and Claudine Wirths. *Are You My Type? Or Why Aren't You More Like Me?* Palo Alto, CA: Consulting Psychologists Press, 1992.

Boyer, Ernest L. "Art as Language: Its Place in the Schools," *Beyond Creating: The Place for Art in America's Schools.* 1985.

Brendtro, Larry, Martin Brokenleg and Steve Van Bockern. *Reclaiming Youth At Risk: Our Hope for the Future.* Bloomington, IN: National Education Service, 1990.

Brewer, Chris and Don Campbell. *Rhythms of Learning.* Tucson, AZ: Zephyr Press, 1991.

Brooks, Jacqueline Grennon. "Teachers and Students: Constructivists Forging New Connections," *Educational Leadership.* February 1990.

Brookes, Mona. *Drawing with Children.* Los Angeles: Tarcher, 1986.

Bry, Adelaide. *Visualization: Directing the Movies of Your Mind.* New York: Harper & Row, 1978.

Butler, Kathleen. *It's All in Your Mind.* Columbia, CT: The Learner's Dimension, 1986.

Butler, Kathleen. *Learning and Teaching in Style.* Columbia, CT: The Learner's Dimension, 1986.

Buzan, Tony. *Use Both Sides Of Your Brain.* New York: E.P. Dutton, 1976.

Byham, William. *Zapp! in Education: How Empowerment Can Improve the Quality of Instruction, and Student and Teacher Satisfaction.* New York: Fawcett Columbine, 1992.

Caine, Renate Nummela and Geoffrey. *Making Connections: Teaching and the Human Brain.* Alexandria, VA: ASCD, 1991.

Cairn, Rich and James Kielsmeier. *Growing Hope: A Sourcebook on Integrating Youth Service into the School Curriculum.* Roseville, MN: National Youth Leadership Council, 1991.

Calvin, William. *The Cerebral Symphony.* New York: Bantam Books, 1990.

Campbell, Don. *100 Ways to Improve Teaching Using Your Voice & Music.* Tucson, AZ: Zephyr Press, 1992.

Capacchione, Lucia. *The Creative Journal for Children.* Boston: Shambhala, 1989.

Carbo, Marie, Kenneth Dunn and Rita Dunn. *Teaching Students to Read Through Their Individualized Learning Strengths.* Englewood Cliffs: Prentice Hall, 1986.

Cherry, Clare, Douglas Godwin, and Jesse Staples. *Is the Left Brain Always Right?* Belmont, CA: David S. Lake Publishers, 1989.

Clarke, Jean Illsley. *Self-Esteem, A Family Affair.* Minneapolis: Winston Press, 1978.

Cohen, Elizabeth. *Designing Groupwork.* New York: Teachers College Press, 1986.

Covey, Stephen. *The 7 Habits of Highly Effective People.* New York: Simon & Schuster, 1989.

Creative Publications. *WorkMat Math: Thinking Through Story Problems and Story Problems on Their Own; TOPS (Techniques of Problem Solving); "Math With Pizzazz.* Palo Alto, CA: Creative Publications.

Dodd, Anne Wescott. *A Parent's Guide to Innovative Education.* Chicago, IL: Noble Press, 1992.

Ellison, Launa. "Positive Self Talk." *Teaching K-8,* August/Sept. 1987.

Espeland, Pamela and Rosemary Wallner. *Making the Most of Today.* Minneapolis: Free Spirit Publishing, 1991.

Fadiman, Dorothy. *Why Do These Kids Love School?* (PBS video special.) Menlo Park, CA: Concentric Media, 1991.

Fanning, Patrick. *Visualization for Change.* Oakland, CA: New Harbinger Publications, 1988.

Fiske, Edward. *Smart Schools, Smart Kids: Why Do Some Schools Work?* New York: Simon & Schuster, 1991.

Forester, Anne and Margaret Reinhard. *The Learner's Way.* Winnipeg, Canada: Peguis, 1989.

Gardner, Howard. *Frames of Mind: The Theory of Multiple Intelligences.* New York: Basic Books, 1983.

Gardner, Howard. *Multiple Intelligences: The Theory in Practice, A Reader.* New York: Basic Books, 1993.

Gardner, Howard. *The Unschooled Mind: How Children Think and How Schools Should Teach.* New York: Basic Books, 1991.

Gilligan, Carol. *In A Different Voice.* Cambridge, MA: Harvard University Press, 1982.

Glasser, William. *Control Theory.* New York: Harper & Row, 1984.

Glasser, William. *Control Theory in the Classroom.* New York: Harper & Row, 1986.

Glasser, William. *The Quality School.* New York: Harper & Row, 1990.

Goodlad, John. *A Place Called School.* New York: McGraw-Hill, 1984.

Grinder, John and Richard Bandler. *The Structure of Magic II.* Palo Alto, CA: Science and Behavior Books, 1976.

Guilford, J.P. *Way Beyond the IQ,* and all *Structure of Intellect (SOI)* materials. El Segundo, CA: Creative Education Foundation, 1977.

Hart, Leslie. *Human Brain and Human Learning.* New York: Longman, 1983.

Heacox, Diane. *Up From Under-Achievement.* Minneapolis: Free Spirit Publishing, 1991.

Healy, Jane. *Your Child's Growing Mind: A Guide to Learning and Brain Development from Birth to Adolescence.* New York: Doubleday, 1987.

Healy, Jane. *Endangered Minds: Why Our Children Don't Think.* New York: Simon and Schuster, 1990.

Henderson, Kathy. *What Would We Do Without You? A Guide to Volunteer Activities for Kids.* Minneapolis: Betterway Publications, 1990.

Herman, Gail and Patricia Hollingsworth. *Kinetic Kaleidoscope: Exploring Movement and Energy in the Visual Arts.* Tucson, AZ: Zephyr Press, 1992.

Herrmann, Ned. *The Creative Brain.* Lake Lure, NC: The Brain Dominance Institute.

Hilke, Eileen. *Cooperative Learning.* Bloomington, IN: Phi Delta Kappa.

Hutchison, Michael. *Megabrain.* New York: William Morrow, 1986.

Humphreys, James. *Teaching Children to Relax.* Springfield, IL: Charles Thomas Publishing, 1988.

Hunter, Madeline. *Mastery Teaching.* El Segundo, CA: TIP Publications, 1988.

Interact Simulation Games. Lakeside, CA.

Johnson, David and Roger Johnson. *Cooperation and Competition: Theory and Research.* Edina, MN: Interaction Book Co., 1990.

Johnson, Lee. *If I Ran the Family.* Minneapolis: Free Spirit Publishing, 1992.

Justice, Blair. *Who Gets Sick: Thinking and Health.* Houston, TX: Peak Press, 1987.

Keirsey, David and Marilyn Bates. *Please Understand Me.* Del Mar, CA: Prometheus Nemesis Books, 1978.

Kline, Peter. *The Everyday Genius.* Arlington, VA: Great Ocean Publishers, 1988.

Kline, Peter and Laurence Martel. *School Success.* Arlington, VA: Great Ocean Publishers, 1992.

Kovalik, Susan. *ITI: The Model, Integrated Thematic Instruction.* Oak Creek, AZ: Books for Educators, 1993.

K-SOS (a subtest of *K-ABC*). Circle Pines, MN: American Guidance Service.

Lazarus, Arnold. *In the Mind's Eye: The Power of Imagery for Personal Enrichment.* New York: Guilford Press, 1977.

Lazear, David. *Seven Ways of Knowing.* Palatine, IL: Skylight Publishing, 1991.

Lazear, David. *Seven Ways of Teaching.* Palatine, IL: Skylight Publishing, 1992.

Lawrence, Gordon. *People Types and Tiger Stripes.* Palo Alto, CA: Center for Applications of Psychological Type, 1982.

Learning Style Profile. Reston, VA: National Association of Secondary School Principals.

Learning Styles Network Newsletter. Jamaica, NY.

Lewis, Barbara. *Kids with Courage: True Stories About Young People Making A Difference.* Minneapolis: Free Spirit Publishing, 1991.

Lewis, Barbara. *The Kid's Guide to Social Action.* Minneapolis: Free Spirit Publishing, 1991.

Lions Quest Skills for Adolescence. Granville, OH.

Macaulay, David. *The Way Things Work.* Boston: Houghton Mifflin, 1988.

"Making New Friends" (a reproducible activity page). *Learning 88*, September, 1988.

Margulies, Nancy. *Mapping Inner Space.* Tucson, AZ: Zephyr Press, 1991.

Maslow, Abraham. *Toward a Psychology of Being.* New York: Litton Educational Publishing, 1968.

Mason, Kathy. *Beyond Words: The Art and Practice of Visual Thinking.* Tucson, AZ: Zephyr Press, 1991.

McGinnis, Ellen and Arnold Goldstein. *Skill-Streaming the Elementary School Child.* Champaign, IL: Research Press Co., 1984.

McGuinness, Diane. *When Children Don't Learn.* New York: Basic Books, 1985.

McCarthy, Bernice. *The 4Mat System: Teaching to Learning Styles with Right/Left Mode Techniques.* Barrington, IL: EXCEL, Inc., 1981, 1987.

McCarthy, Bernice and S. Leflar. *4MAT In Action.* Oak Brook, IL: EXCEL, Inc., 1988.

McCarthy, Bernice. "Using the 4MAT System to Bring Learning Styles to Schools." *Educational Leadership*, October 1990.

McConnell, James. *Understanding Human Behavior.* New York: Holt, Rinehart and Winston, 1986.

McKim, Robert. *Thinking Visually.* Belmont, CA: Lifetime Learning Publications, 1980.

Meisgeier, Murphy and Meisgeier. *A Teacher's Guide to Type.* Palo Alto, CA: CPP, 1989.

"The Mind in Motion." *Discover* Magazine. No. 13, Winter 1990-91.

Modality Kit: "A Common Sense Approach to Learning" (filmstrip). Columbus, OH: Zaner-Bloser.

Moir, Anne and David Jessel. *BrainSex.* London, England: Mandarin, 1989.

More, Arthur. *Learning Styles and Indian Students: A Review of Research.* ERIC Document Ed 249 028, 1984.

Murphy, Elizabeth. *I Am A Good Teacher* (a skit). Palo Alto, CA: Center for the Applications of Psychological Type, 1987.

Murphy, Elizabeth. *The Murphy-Meisgeier Type Indicator for Children (MMTIC).* Palo Alto, CA: Consulting Psychologists Press, 1990.

Murphy, Elizabeth. *The Developing Child.* Palo Alto, CA: Consulting Psychologists Press, 1992.

Myers, Isabel Briggs. *Gifts Differing.* Palo Alto, CA: Consulting Psychologists Press, 1980.

Myers, Isabel Briggs and Mary H McCaulley. *Manual: A Guide to the Development and Use of the Myers-Briggs Type Indicator.* Palo Alto, CA: Consulting Psychologists Press, 1986.

Oakes, Jeannie and Martin Lipton. *Making the Best of Schools.* New Haven, CT: Yale University Press, 1990.

Packer, Alex. *Bringing Up Parents.* Minneapolis: Free Spirit Publishing, 1992.

Perry, Susan. *Playing Smart.* Minneapolis: Free Spirit Publishing, 1990.

Practical Intelligence for Schools. New Haven, CT: Yale University, Dept. of Psychology.

Purkey, William and John Novak. *Inviting School Success.* Belmont, CA: Wadsworth Publishing, 1987.

Radencich, Marguerite and Jeanne Schumm. *How To Help Your Child with Homework.* Minneapolis: Free Spirit Publishing, 1988.

Rich, Dorothy. *MegaSkills.* Boston: Houghton Mifflin, 1988.

Rico, Gabriele Lussser. *Writing the Natural Way*. Los Angeles: Tarcher, 1983.

Roberts, Gail and Lorraine Guttormson. *You and Your Family: A Survival Guide for Adolescence*. Minneapolis: Free Spirit Publishing, 1990.

Roberts, Gail and Lorraine Guttormson. *You and School: A Survival Guide for Adolescence*. Minneapolis: Free Spirit Publishing, 1990.

Roberts, Gail and Lorraine Guttormson. *You and Stress: A Survival Guide for Adolescence*. Minneapolis: Free Spirit Publishing, 1990.

Roberts, Gail and Lorraine Guttormson. *Leader's Guide to the Series: A Survival Guide for Adolescence*. Minneapolis: Free Spirit Publishing, 1990.

Rogers, Carl. *Freedom to Learn*. Columbus, OH: Charles Merrill, 1969.

Rose, Laura. *Picture This: Teaching Reading Through Visualization*. Tucson, AZ: Zephyr Press, 1989.

Rosenfield, Israel. *The Invention of Memory*. New York: Basic Books, 1988.

Safer, Morley. "Reading By the Colors." *60 Minutes*, CBS News, August 20, 1989.

Schmidt, Fran and Alice and Friedman. *Creative Conflict Solving for Kids*. Miami Beach, FL: Grace Contrino Adams Peace Education Foundation, 1986.

"Shy Folk May Be Shy of Dopamine." *BrainMind Bullletin*, Nov. 1987.

Sinatra, Richard. *Visual Literacy Connections to Thinking, Reading and Writing*. Springfield, IL: Charles Thomas, 1986.

Sizer, Ted. *Horace*. Providence, RI: Brown University.

Slavin, Robert. *Cooperative Learning*. New York: Longman, 1983.

Sperry, Roger. "Consciousness, Personal Identity, and the Divided Brain." *The Dual Brain*. New York: Guilford, 1985.

Spier, Peter. *People*. New York: Doubleday, 1990.

Springer, Sally and Georg Deutch. *Left Brain, Right Brain*. New York: W.H.Freeman, 1985.

Strauss, Susan and Pamela Espeland. *Sexual Harassment for Teens*. Minneapolis: Free Spirit Publishing, 1992.

Student Learning Styles and Brain Behavior. Reston, VA: National Association of Secondary School Principals, 1982.

Sylwester, Robert. *A Celebration of Neurons: An Educator's Guide to the Human Brain*. Alexandria, VA: ASCD, 1995.

TenHouten, Warren. "Cerebral-Lateralization Theory and the Sociology of Knowledge." *The Dual Brain*. New York: Guilford, 1985.

Tobias, Cindy and Pat Guild. *No Sweat, How To Use Your Learning Style To Be A Better Student*. Seattle, WA: The Teaching Advisory, 1986.

Waas, Lane Longino. *Imagine That!* Rolling Hills Estate: Jalmar Press, 1991.

Wheelock, Anne. *Crossing the Tracks: How "Untracking" Can Save America's Schools*. New York: The New Press, 1992.

Wilson, John. *The Invitational Elementary Classroom*. Springfield, IL: Charles Thomas Publishing, 1986.

Wood, George. *Schools That Work: America's Most Innovative Public Education Programs*. New York: Dutton, 1992.

Index